# MULTIPLICITY

*How to Unlock the Five Freedoms and*

*Create Unlimited Abundance in Every*

*Part of Your Life*

## BY

## JOE EVANGELISTI

Ordering Information: Quantity sales. Special discounts are available on quantity purchases by corporations, associations, and others. Orders by U.S. trade bookstores and wholesalers.

DREAMSTARTERS

www.DreamStartersPublishing.com

# Table of Contents

# Introduction

People know me as the *Wholescaling* entrepreneur, author, and business investor.  What they don't know is all those things are a product of what I really always wanted, FREEDOM.  You are reading this book, so it's a good guess you want the same things. To understand how I came to write it, you should know my back story.

Let me be clear with you -- the *art of the pivot* is my back story. How did I get here? Why do I do what I do? Where do I come from and how did I get my bumps along the road? And how is this story going to chart a course that will help you realize what your true potential as a leader is?

It all started with my love for construction.  I've been in construction my whole life. My father was a general contractor, a drywall contractor turned house-builder and, as soon as I was able to walk, I was practically attached to his knee, dragged around job sites because I was afraid of falling in a hole. By the time I was old enough to throw drywall scraps in the dumpster and broom-sweep the floor, it was in my blood. I loved construction.

I was lucky enough to meet a foreman my father had working for him right after I graduated High School. He was a Senior Chief reservist in the US Navy Seabees (The United

States Navy Construction Battalions). At the time, I didn't know what that was or that I was being called to serve.

When I met the Senior Chief, he pointed out that I could enlist and be a builder. He explained what the Seabees were and that I could do construction in the Navy. I was lucky as most people don't know this construction battalion even exists. They build forward operating bases, support the Marines, and defend a new base until the troops come in. I was sold!

Basically, we're fighting, construction-men. Our motto is "We build, we fight!" I did that for six years and loved it. I got to see the world, had amazing experiences, and was fortunate to get the desire for travel out of my system.

I readjusted to civilian life quickly in 2004 and 2005, ending up in New Jersey. I met my wife right after I got out of the Navy, ending up where I started. I wasn't holding dad's knee this time, I was running the general contracting department for him.

Still, I wanted something bigger! I thought to myself now that I have all the construction knowledge I could have in the world, what does everybody do?

*"Everyone tells you the same thing: If you want to be rich, you have to get into real estate. That's where the riches are."*

So I hopped into flipping with the intention of grinding it out. I was comfortable and confident with the construction aspect of the things, but I had to figure out how to buy the homes, how to structure deals, how to protect assets in partnerships and LLCs, and all the things that have nothing to do with hammers and nails.

Turns out I jumped in at what I now call The Lucky Time. Lucky because it was in 2007 when I bought my first property, which was right before the real estate market imploded.

If I had gotten in three years earlier, I would have gotten away with making terrible decisions and mistakes. Why? Because the market would have let me and still survive.

Instead, I got in at a time where none of that was possible. I took all of my savings and all of the money I had earned in the military and started plunking it into real estate thinking this is the gold rush.

What happened in the first two or three deals that we did? The market softened almost immediately. It didn't crash just yet, but it definitely softened. Where we thought a project would sell for 320K, it dropped to 260K almost overnight. Instead of cashing out of our first few deals for big money and becoming an overnight success, I turned into an overnight Landlord instead. Not really how I planned it.

This is where I learned the art of the pivot. I began picking up different means OF EARNING. I became a Realtor and started selling different properties for a commission. This is what real estate investors do: Go get their licenses and then they'll be able to figure out stuff along the way.

In the middle of all this, I quit general contracting and dove headfirst all-in. I said to myself that I have to make this work. So I just started flipping houses full-time. It was scary, but I knew that I was passionate about it, so I cut that safety net. Pretty quickly, we accumulated three flips that we did all by hand. Only one problem, I couldn't sell them.

There were bills to be paid and my wife was depending on me, even though luckily she had a job. But it wasn't like we were making big money. I had to get myself a commission job and figure out how to start selling, and that's when I started to become a realtor and sell the property as well as figure out how to piece stuff together.

I pressed on for three, four, five years when it all started to come to a head and became a pressure situation for me. I'm a realtor, very successful in the office where I was working my way up with lots of clients. It didn't come naturally because while I've always been good at talking to people, that's a little different than actually turning them into clients and closing sales. I leaned into my strength, which was construction knowledge, which is why people listened to me.

But again, it was all work ethic as I was driven towards it. When I used to tell this story, I called it the Superman story because I would get up in the morning and put on a suit and tie and dress up so that I could go to work prepared. I would prospect, set appointments, call and set up listing appointments to meet a certain quota each day, call my buyers back and set up appointments for the weekend, set up my open houses. Whatever I had to do. I would get all of that work in before noon, so I would be at the office by 7:30 am, on the phone by 9 o'clock, and by noon I would have it all set up. I would get in the car, get home, have lunch, and it would be like Superman in the phone booth as I flipped off the suit and put on jeans and a t-shirt, headed to the Jobsite, and became the contractor. I would show up with paint samples and tiles and even pick up toilets at Home Depot if I had to, run schedules and carry a checkbook in my back pocket. Because God forbid if a sub was there and I didn't have any money for him, so I had to keep everything organized.

The reason I call it the *Superman story* is not because I was Superman. I was probably the opposite of Superman. I was trying to be Superman, trying to be everything to everybody, but internally I was falling apart. So I thought there was conflict when the reality of it was all in my head.

The more I started becoming my unique self, the more I stopped caring what other people thought. That's when the changes all occurred. Part of the problem was I was putting on this fake front for myself. It was all bullshit because I'd be finding stuff to do to keep me sitting in the office till 8 p.m., stuff that I didn't need to do at all. And when a day comes up that I'm not busy, I start feeling like I'm not accomplishing anything. What does it mean for my self-esteem if I come to work and there is not a lot to do, or maybe I'm not functioning properly? Maybe I've got to pay closer attention and find problems to solve. That just creates problems.

*"I thought one day it will happen. How many of us chase that one day?"*

I had to make a pivot and decide how to make the change. I started investing in coaching and mentorship. I became the person who unlocked freedom – rather than just a person wishing for it.

Once I started to see the rewards come to life, I realized the lessons I applied needed to be shared with the world. That's why I wrote this book: You get to hear it from someone who has personally applied these lessons to accomplish the things you are chasing. I've actually done it. I'm not just posting fake stories about it (like so many "gurus" on social media). If you are ready to start creating time and opportunities, **Multiplicity** is for you.

Dial in these ingredients and it will be the key to unlocking the Five Freedoms.

# Chapter 1

# The Five Freedoms

Let's face it: Financial freedom is a simple concept and the only free people typically talk about. And this is part of the problem: When you hear people talk about their goals, they concentrate on money. Why is their goal not time freedom or geographical freedom?

When my coach started laying out the Five Freedoms to me, I was shocked there even are *Five* Freedoms in the first place. I used to think that if I had financial freedom, I could create all the rest. But it is the antithesis. It is these others that are going to start creating your financial freedom.

If you were like me, before reading this book, you believed that if you had enough money, you could make anything happen. This is why when I take on a new student I coach backward. If you ask somebody what is their goal, what do you think they are going to say? Make $100,000 this year, travel, invest in this, buy that, do this, do that... it's all money, money, money. It's always money.

When I tell them to put together ten Centers of Improvement, or COIs, ninety percent list all ten as business goals. Buy some equipment, expand my sales team, increase my marketing, take on another territory, you name it! It's all business. Then I'll take it back and ask if they have kids or a wife, and shouldn't those be your goals? When was the last time they had a conversation with their wife to find out what she wants?

Then you get the defensive answers like, "of course I have kids, who else am I doing this for?" You're trying to expand to other territories for your kids? Do you want to hire a marketing manager for your kids? Or growing the legal department for your wife? What does that do for her? When was the last time you asked her about what matters to her?

So we start to dial it back into these freedoms and people start to realize that they're chasing the wrong shit, which gets right back to the chasing. Why are we chasing anything when we should be creating an outcome that fits our lifestyle?

Of course, it's completely different for everybody. I have clients who want to create an automatic lifestyle where they can live on a sailboat. That's a lifestyle totally different than mine, but it is their dream. The family is on board, the

11

kids are homeschooled, and all he needs are a sailboat and Wi-Fi. Nothing wrong with doing that, so let's make that outcome a reality and we're halfway there in three and a half months. That's an outcome worth chasing.

The problem is that people focus on business goals and ultimately look at financial freedom only. Passive income, retirement funds, a million fucking dollars a year in income. Okay, good. Why? For what? What is it going to create for you? Let's say you get it, now what? If that is what you want, sure, you can have that. Without understanding the purpose of this Financial Freedom, I promise you it will be an empty achievement.

## *FINANCIAL FREEDOM*

Financial freedom is self-explanatory: make more money than you spend. What we are trying to create with Multiplicity is similar to how we are trying to multiply a team where great leaders create great leaders, once the foundation and the framework have been set. So it is the same thing with what you want to accomplish with your money. It isn't just making more money than you can spend, but also multiplying the outcome of your money. It's about creating an amazing stream of income, then taking that income and creating another amazing stream of income. And then another amazing stream of income, and another, and another... and starting to create multiple facets of income. Do they say the rich have more than eight streams of income? I got news for you: Some of the wealthiest people in the world have a hundred streams of income. So many that they lose track of all the streams.

It's all because of multiplicity. When you become great at utilizing money, you leverage money to create more money. You invest in businesses with passive income or people with passive income or opportunities with passive income. Ultimately, you create a family office that has passive income in all different directions, and you manage the money and make it work for you. It's not outside of the reach of most entrepreneurs. The only reason many don't achieve it is they don't even think about it.

Most entrepreneurs think about how much money they can make within their existing business each year. It is not about that at all. Think instead about how much money you put to work for yourself each year.

You could make $200,000 a year and be a multi-fucking-millionaire in ten years. Or, you could make a million dollars each year and be broke as fuck in ten years.

You have to be a good steward of money and also understand that money is like fairy dust – it doesn't exist. Nobody has any cash on them. Of course, I carry cash in my pocket because it makes me feel good about myself, but nobody honestly has a million dollars of cash.

13

We're trading cryptocurrency right now. It's all fairy dust, nothing but ones and zeros in space. Just a number on a computer somewhere that isn't even yours. If you have $100,000 in your bank account, try going to the bank and take it out. They don't have that shit on them!

Do you want proof it's not real? The US has created more money in the last twelve months than existed in the world since the inception of the concept of money. Ever! But where is it all at? It simply doesn't exist.

What separates truly wealthy people is knowing how to multiply it. They know how to create it, versus creating insufficiencies. Bad debt versus good debt, rich debt versus poor debt, and so on. They utilize this principle on steroids.

This is how you truly create Financial Freedom.

## TIME FREEDOM

When most people hear "Time Freedom", they think of doing whatever they want at any time. In their mind, it looks like a blank calendar they get to fill in however they want. Sit on an island beach all day with an umbrella drink in their hand and waves lapping on the white sand.

Why? Because they associate Time Freedom with having Financial Freedom, which means they can do whatever they want. Get a tan, listen to the birds' chirp, whatever.

Newsflash: Nobody and I mean *nobody* who is wealthy could do that for more than a day or two. They would be bored out of their fucking minds in five days. You may want to think about that as a dreamscape, but the reality is true time freedom is learning how to control the clock so that you can do things when you want to do them. It doesn't mean you don't do them at all. It means they get done on your scheduled time, instead of someone else's.

If you want to sleep in till 10 am, that's your deal. If you want to work on the weekends and take off Tuesdays through Fridays, that's what you do. True-time freedom is doing things when you want to. It is not having anything at all to do.

People who have a 9-to-5 might think financial freedom means quitting their job and kicking up their feet without doing anything. Think about it, you would be so bored within a week or two! Think about our basic human needs. We would immediately cut out growth and contribution. Important needs which we will touch upon soon enough. They won't get any significance or uncertainty or variety when you are not doing anything.

In that position, people will immediately find themselves in depression. Take the example of someone who has a sudden rush of money, winning the lottery, or an inheritance. They tend to lose sight of the variety or the significance which made things interesting and challenging for them before the money. Some of it just goes away overnight, and people won't

15

realize that it wasn't the money that did it for them, it was the change in their lives and circumstances, and the absence of the drive to do anything that put them where they find themselves now.

Understand that Time Freedom is the exact opposite of having nothing to do! Instead is controlling your time so you get more of the things that are important to you do. This will lead to more fulfillment and help you gain access to the other four freedoms.

Radical Calendar Management = Time Freedom

## *GEOGRAPHICAL FREEDOM*

The name might suggest it, but this isn't just being anywhere you, please. That is part of it, of course, and pretty self-explanatory. If you have an RV with Wi-Fi access, you can run your company on Zoom. We all have smartphones so you can simply get on a call with as many people as possible. Technology makes geographical freedom so much different today than twenty years ago.

To take a personal example, my entire team is virtual. I'm looking to hire an executive assistant right now and I don't care where they're based. There are things with geographical freedom technology has allowed us, which didn't exist twenty years ago. The American Dream – which once used to be about buying a house and living there for sixty years, paying it off in thirty, saving up the rest of the money, and retiring to start traveling – has now shifted by the current generation to simply renting everything they need wherever they go.

They can have the same amount of money and save it as they go but have these mini-vacations. You can thank Tim Ferriss for this as he mentioned in his book "The Four Hour Workweek" that I could just have these mini-retirements, so why would I need to wait till I get old, fat, and out of shape to go travel if I can do all of that when I'm thirty? I want to enjoy my life while I'm young enough to enjoy it, which is great.

That is geographical freedom. This new generation made that happen and I think our generation was the one that kind of even knew it existed and started it.

Geographical freedom also expands your mindset and allows you to grow. When you go to different places it enhances your uncertainty and variety. Let's say you live in the North-East, as I do, and it's 22 degrees and snowing outside. You could have the best and most productive day. I mean, take it from me, I could be kicking ass and taking names. If you pick me up and put me in the Four Seasons in West Palm Beach, do you think I am more productive or less productive? Believe me, I'm going to be *more* productive. Destinations like these drive me. Those experiences shift you. Sometimes you hop on a plane and you start getting your best ideas. New environments change you. Geographical freedom, whether you talk about productivity levels or just mindset, is

17

expanding your mind and growth. That movement is allowing you to think differently. It's allowing you to see things differently and allowing you to talk to different people to get different opinions from different areas. You aren't just stuck in your little bubble this way. Geographical freedom allows you to create and create quicker.

## FREEDOM OF PURPOSE

Most people don't know this exists! Even when they do, they have the hardest time figuring out how to relate to it. It's like speaking Latin. "Freedom of purpose? Why would I want to have freedom of purpose?" Well, what *is* your purpose? What are you here for?

Ask this: What do you want? Here are the answers: "Um, I don't know what I want." It is a tough question to answer, what you want to create or experience, or what you want out of life.

It hit home for me three years ago. We were flipping 80 to 90 houses a year. My partner and I sat down to meet and something clicked for me (this at a time I didn't even know the definition of freedom of purpose).

I asked him what the goals were for the following year. It was a doldrums thing we used to do every year. "Do you want to do 120 houses?" he asked, and I'm like, "Dude, I don't even want to do fucking 80 again!" It was miserable! Sure, we made money but I had never been so beaten.

We had a ton of people on my team that I didn't even like, people in the office that I didn't even know, hiring people that wouldn't settle into the culture because the culture stunk. I created an environment that I didn't like being in, so much so I didn't even want to come to the office anymore.

I'll be honest, I was a bad leader, a bad visionary, I avoided being in the environment because I had created this big machine that churned and burned and built houses and flipped them. Everyone was good at their jobs, we were making money and doing alright, but I was not happy. So I looked at my partner and he looked at me, and once I told him I didn't even want to do 80 again, he said "I don't want to either."

And that was a freaking slap in the face, a right hook that McGregor would take. I realized that son of a bitch, we're losing! I think we're taking a loss and we need to go back into training. Reset the clock and pivot once more.

It wasn't that things weren't working, or we weren't making money, or that people weren't getting paid, or even that we weren't creating. It just wasn't fulfilling, and it wasn't fulfilling me. Not me, or my partner, or anyone else. So what the fuck was the point?

We weren't creating a good culture. People were coming in and out like a revolving door. There are some people I liked, some I didn't like, some I didn't like *at all*, some I didn't even know, some I didn't care to know, and I just wasn't a good leader. So I reset the clock at that moment and said to him, "What about a different industry?"

I think it happened to me once on a retreat I went to in Malibu about three years ago. I was on a rooftop deck at a hotel overlooking the beach. Again, this is where I get my expansion mindset from, and I remember thinking to myself I needed to do something different. What about bigger, what about better? What about self-storage? If I did that, the numbers were so much more vast.

It was scary. A laundry list of questions I didn't have answers to need them. I had no idea how I would get investors involved. I didn't even know who I needed to talk to. Where did a deal like this even start? Let me call my engineer, my attorney, or whoever to find out if anyone was selling any piece of land like that. And that was the catalyst, the piece that sparked it.

I started realizing if I moved in this direction, I could keep some of the key players that I loved on the team, The rest would be better off, they weren't fulfilling their purpose in our company anyway.

*"Keep your aces in their places."*

I had a couple of aces in my sleeve back then but a lot of jokers. So I was going to keep the aces but getting rid of the jokers because I didn't need them. They were just there taking up payroll, and my payroll was big.

I could do ten self-storages a year with a quarter of the payroll. I would keep my aces. I could surround myself with people I loved, people that I truly wanted to grow with.

If I was going to be 80 years old on a porch smoking a cigar and drinking a whisky and talking about how we dominated the fucking self-storage industry and made a billion dollars, these were the kind of people I would want with me. A smaller group, stronger tribe, better culture, bigger tribe.

I would do ten deals a year instead of a hundred so I could manage them more easily and create growth. In ten deals, I would do twenty times the revenue created on 80 houses. Now that is a purpose I could stand behind.

This was fucking exciting to me. Keep in mind in the last 80 houses we flipped, I never stepped foot in them. I didn't even know where they were, so I didn't give a fuck. I had no passion, no purpose behind them; I was just doing it. All it was to me was a number. And the problem was the people were a number, too.

That's the kind of asshole I was. They were all numbers. I looked at people like paychecks, income, and expenses and that was it? I don't want to say that I was that cold I didn't care about them, I did care about some, but I wasn't a good visionary or a good leader. I wasn't up to taking charge, and as a matter of fact, I was kind of a spoiled little bitch, because I was making money and thought it earned me the right to be an absentee landlord.

I wouldn't say I wasn't proud of the company because we had a good product. It wasn't a question of pride, it was just that I wasn't in love with the process, nor did I have a purpose behind it. Don't get me wrong, we built great houses and our people were doing great work. The internals wasn't broken at all, but it just wasn't in alignment with who I wanted to be.

That's when I figured out that my purpose isn't behind this thing. I wasn't surrounded by people I liked doing business with. I had a couple of people that I liked and my business partner was the guy who was my best friend since I was ten years old, so we were cool with each other. But it ended up becoming me and him running everything and taking on all the responsibilities, even afraid to give any responsibility away because the guys to who we were giving it to were going to drop the ball and that caused us to not trust them. We were micromanaging everything and it just wasn't turning out to be good management at that point. That's when I made that key decision that this could be so much better, which became the purpose-driven piece of this shift.

Now it was no longer going to be about WHAT we were doing. It was going to be about building off our PURPOSE and the RESULTS we were after first in order to reverse engineer WHO we wanted to join us for the journey.

## FREEDOM OF RELATIONSHIPS

This is probably my favorite of the Five Freedoms, and with Freedom of Purpose, the hardest to master. In my tribe now, quite a few people understand what Freedom of Purpose and Relationships means and have these because I've cut it down to only those people who have them. But when I take on new coaching clients, they have never even heard of these things. This is one of those game shifters – purpose and relationships – that shift the entire dichotomy of people's mindsets and stories.

Relationships are an individual thing as you have to define who are the people who are lifting you and who are holding you down. This is where we set standards when we talk about The Four Ss soon. And one of those is Standards: What are the standards that I set for myself, and how am I going to hold myself in a relationship? In relationships, I only engage in what I call ten-year relationships. What that means is that if I'm spending more than ten minutes with you, it is because I believe I will be talking to you in ten years, or I believe that there is an opportunity that we should be talking about in ten years. I think that we are going to build together and be talking together in ten years because I don't want to waste any time with you if I don't think you're going to help me grow or if I can't help you grow. It has to be a mutually beneficial relationship as you're there to support me or grow with me, or you're there to grow next to me, alongside me.

And if one of those three things is not true, there is no reason for us to waste time. My time is way too valuable and I am not afraid to say that anymore. I spent 15 years being afraid to say that every time someone would come up to ask me if they could pick my brains or buy me a coffee. I just had a guy talk to me on the phone for fifteen minutes last week – nice guy, by the way – offering to buy me a steak dinner with wine, whatever it took. Dude, just book a fucking phone call! People think that going out to dinner is no big deal, but it sure is a fucking huge deal! Do you think taking time away from my eight and eleven-year-old kids isn't a big deal? Every minute I spend with them is precious, and I don't know what I'm going to miss or know what they did in school today. I don't know what my daughter is going to say to me and make me learn, or shock me, or surprise me, or even amaze me. Do you honestly think I am going to waste that on someone I have never even met? It doesn't matter what steak you buy me or even the most expensive bottle of wine on the menu, I don't give a shit. That is not worth missing my kids' smiles, plain and simple.

And that is Freedom of Relationships. So many people have this hardship of letting go, which is all mindset-based because we're selling ourselves in the past. My past has defined me that I'm a nice guy, and nice has nothing to do with it. Just because I am a nice guy, doesn't mean that I can't protect my time. So this guy, for example, I gave him fifteen minutes of my time and spoke to him, talked to him, asked him where he was going and where he wanted to go, gave him a couple of tips and tricks, gave him some exercises to do. He followed up with me in a message and said that "Holy crap, man. In fifteen minutes, I didn't even think I was going to have takeaways let alone lessons let alone homework. Like, you changed my whole week and my outcome. I'm working on that stuff right now and will get back to you with the feedback." Just a fifteen-minute call.

Just imagine what you could do if you spent your time wisely and created a real impact. And not to brag or anything, but to me, this is a contribution. Instead of letting someone suck time away or waste your time or "take you out to coffee," what would happen if you just asked them what exactly they wanted to talk about? Let's just cut to the chase and not beat around the bush. Do you want to learn about my e-commerce stores? Cool, how about a phone call, I can tell you all about them in ten minutes, and you can invest in them if you want. If you don't, that's cool too because I am not tied to the outcome. That is exactly why I want to be around people with whom I see myself working ten years from now.

That being said, I am allergic to negativity. It's one thing to joke about shit or have an opinion, but if somebody asks me for my time, I just need to go to their social media and see that they're bitching about something like waiting in line at the grocery store or getting a flat tire or about whatever happened to them at work today. They will not be getting five seconds of my time. If you are a timewaster or a complainer or a complainer or a moaner, or just plain negative all the time, I will subconsciously shut you out. My subconscious muscle has been programmed for so long that when I see negativity, I am repulsed by it. I go through my Facebook feed and unfollow or unfriend people constantly because of negativity. I don't even care about your political views as you could be one way or the other, that's not even it. It's just the negativity. If you are a consistent bitcher then you are out of my life. So if you are asking me for my time and the first thing I see on your social media is you complaining about something, there is no chance whatsoever of us working together. Those people do not make it to my life, my wall, and they sure as shit do not make it to my team. That stuff is contagious and you have to cut it out of your life.

*"You will make within $2000 or $3000 of the average of the five people you are surrounded with."*

**Les Brown**

That is part of Freedom of Relationships, asking what relationships you want. And forget about the money aspect of it for a second. Let's talk about social standing or status or how they fit into the six human needs. Are the five people who are surrounding you contributing to growth or charity? Are they volunteering or helping lift other people up? Are they giving out free speeches or sharing knowledge? I believe that you have a moral obligation to share what you know. If you know something that you can help other people grow from, then you have to share that shit. You can't hold it in because if you do, you are hindering other people's growth by not teaching it. Not only that, as a result, you're also hindering your growth by not teaching it. Because here is what happens when you teach, you learn it better.

**The first thing I teach the people that I coach is that after they get the lesson they just learned, their homework is to teach it to somebody.** It is not going to get into their cerebellum until they teach it to someone else, and once they do, it is game-changing. It's a different shift like you're on the other side of the mirror now. All of a sudden you are passing it on to someone else and your contribution level is going up, so you are pushing to another place. It is all part of the factor.

Oftentimes, people are tied to this ball and chain with relationships because of one of the Ten Universal Saboteurs, which we will be looking at in detail as well. One of these is the People Pleaser, and a lot of people fall into this category because ultimately, we're taught to be nice people and be cordial, say thank you, open doors, pull out chairs. What that leads to over time is the cultural buildup that we just have to be nice. Last week, I had this experience with one of my clients who told me that people brought him deals that he can tell at first glance instantly that they are bad deals. But just because he is such a People Pleaser, he thanks them for bringing the deal over, and will just review and get back to them about it. So how do we shift that thinking? Here's how: By saying that you appreciate bringing this deal, but I want to see you win and be successful. When you bring me a deal, I want this to be a joint venture opportunity. We pay out six figures on joint venture opportunities most of the time. So I record a forty-five-minute training inside of our self-storage group on exactly how to find joint venture opportunities, and what I would like you to do is spend the forty-five minutes and it's worth every penny of your time since it's free. Go in there, take good notes, and when you bring deals along the next time, you will know if it meets our criteria. Because I don't want to waste your time finding me deals that are in the middle of a cornfield that doesn't meet our criteria. I want you to bring me deals with more meat on the bone so that I know that you can get paid. Doesn't that make more sense?

This way, what I did was I said no *and* lifted you at the same time. And so a People Pleaser just needs to learn how to please people while creating a win-win. It's just a shift in mindset. This way, I built myself an asset. So you can be a great leader *and* a people pleaser, and that is the takeaway. So many people-pleasers work so hard and tell themselves that they have to do what they have to do. That is a rational lie because you're rationalizing all the shit that you don't even need to be doing, thus wasting your time and doing what we call 'brown time' when we talk about the productivity pyramid. In there, you're living in brown time because you're doing shit work and convincing yourself why you're supposed to be doing it. Why? Because you're trying to please people when the reality of it is that if you had stepped up and had played it above the line and did the things you were supposed to be doing as a leader, you would define those expectations. And the person you were trying to please would respect you more as the professional that you are.

# Chapter 2

# Limiting Beliefs

---

Most people think that it's too hard, that they're not smart enough or have what it takes or the right education; ultimately, they believe that they shouldn't be happy because they have no reason to get to the next place in their lives. Maybe they were held back at some point or told their whole life that, for instance, "your father was a plumber, your mother was a schoolteacher, everyone in your family has always had a 9-to-5, and that's what you should be."

*"We are told and sold these stories throughout our lives that this is your place and where you should be. Where you belong."*

So effectively, we grow up with these self-limiting beliefs or self-limiting doubts, and what I started to pay attention to was that I had to go and start to peek behind the curtain of my mind. I had to figure out what was going on with my psychology, how my mindset was dialing it in, what my beliefs were, what my values were. I had to reset the rules that I was playing by, and also had to reset what was possible, because of my mindset that I'm a one-man band. An island. Sure, I have an assistant, but I can do everything myself. So I had to reevaluate and reset all that.

*"The strongest force in the human personality is the need to be consistent with how we define ourselves."*

**Tony Robbins**

That right there shook me. When I heard it, I thought to myself that I'm defined as this person, that this is who I am. I've defined myself in this role, so now I have to change it. We can either define ourselves as a victim and remain that way as a victim, or we can define ourselves as the *victor* and move to victory. Those are the only two options. And if we stay in that story, and if we stay in that limiting belief that we are in, we are going to continue to remain the victim. But if we decide to shift and reset our story, we can start to move towards victory. We can finally start to move towards what it is that we want to

31

accomplish. The big dreams, the big goals; not the day-to-day putting out fires and busywork. Those are tasks. I want to move more towards outcomes. Either way, what I learned from my mentors there was where my focus goes, my energy flows. Back in the day, I would focus on the tasks at hand or what was right in front of me. I would focus on getting the paint or the samples or the tiles or showing the house, nothing that was high-level. What do I want to accomplish? Where do I want to get to? What are my end goals? What do I want my kids to grow up like? How do I want them to be raised? How to even interact with them? What do I want my schedule to look like? How do I want my perfect day to be?

So that's number one: Resetting that mindset. Back in my days in general construction, the perfect day was not what I was thinking about at all. I was thinking about whether to go greige or beige. Does this tile match this wall color? And if I paint it beige, am I going to get a bigger part of the market, or get someone to pay an extra $5,000 for this house? The next level mindset is that if I do this a hundred times a year, what can it do to my teeth? And even ask whether I can get a team to worry about this without ever having to step foot on the property. Up until that point, I had no team or people. This mindset shift created an opportunity where I never even *saw* the last 400 houses that we did before I got out of that business. I never stepped foot on them, or couldn't even tell you where they were. That's the mindset shift, the change that happens. Limiting beliefs will tell you that you have to be the guy who will pick up the wall tile. Getting your mind right – which I call shifting your limiting beliefs or changing your story – will tell you that you can do 400 deals and never set foot on them. That's a shift. Is picking out the tile the best use of my time? Of course not! I'm going to elevate my mindset and my story to become the person that I want to become.

*"The past can only affect if you choose to live there."*

**Tony Robbins**

The past can be this morning, yesterday, last week, ten years ago. You're going to hear a lot of people say that this is where they were brought up, this is what they were taught, this is where they came from, this is what happened to me last year, their girlfriend dumped them, they used to drink a lot but got over that, they used to be overweight and been working out a lot lately. All they tell you is stories about their past. Tell me about today! Tell me about tomorrow. Successful people always talk about the present and the future, not the past. That is visionary shit, and visionaries do not pick out the tile from Home Depot. Visionaries talk about where the team is going and the opportunities they are creating for the people around them. They talk about the stuff that scares them, truly scares them. They can't imagine five years in advance because they can't imagine where their brain is going to take them five years from now. What is my story going to be when I keep resetting it every six months, five years from now? I have no idea because I'm forcing myself to reset and level it up, change my limiting beliefs every step of the way.

With The Four Ss that Unleash Your true potential in an instant, we'll be talking a lot about the ability to bounce back or be bulletproof when it comes to protecting your space and protecting your mindset, protecting *you* as a person. Imagine when you get out of bed the first thing in the morning and you feel vulnerable and at risk. I say this a lot of times that at the first thing in the morning, the last thing you want to be is reactionary. You would rather be proactive, so you'll hear people tell you not to hop out of bed and check your email or phone because nothing good happens in Gmail. No one has ever checked their email and seen that they have won the lottery. No one has ever gone "Yes, finally! I've been waiting for this email!" Nine times out of ten you check your email and you have to just follow up with someone. So you start out trying to bulletproof yourself, and the better your routine at the beginning of the day, the better your mindset, and the better the Four Ss can be bulletproofed at the beginning of your day, the better you can be present during your day. The better you can be grateful during your day. The better your mindset and your power of presence and your effectiveness are going to be during the day. And the better you are going to be able to be at controlling your schedule and doing that high-gain, high-impact activities that you talk about that are going to create high income for you.

## *State - How are you showing up in your mind and body?*

The first of the Four Ss is State, and your State is how you are showing up in your mind and your body. Your physiology has so much control over everything else. For example, if you were in a bad mood or a funk, what do you look like? Your shoulders are slumped over and you're looking down, you have a frown over your face, you're slouching, you're shaky, you probably have low, slow breaths and you're just indifferent to everything around you. If you're in that position and all you do is go for a walk outside or ten jumping jacks or push-ups, you will feel better. You can't take poor physiology and create motion and movement around that, and not feel better. You're putting blood in your bloodstream; you're breathing and opening up. Just try sitting up, push your chest out, pull your shoulders back, straighten your neck, pull your head up. Imagine what it would feel like if you started to pay attention to your posture and physiology. We can create confidence, clarity, and efficiencies just by creating physiology.

Good physiology and good posture can transfer into what we do and how we do one thing is how we do everything. It's the reason why most salespeople make sales calls standing up sometimes. They can put their energy into it just like they would talk to a person one-on-one. A great salesperson isn't sitting on a stool or kicking back in a lounge chair or have their feet up. No one ever sits on a BarcaLounger with a cell phone as a top salesperson. If you ever see a top salesperson, you will see them in a prospecting room or out and about. Most salespeople today are out there in cars or out and about walking and talking. They are erect and have energy going through their body while they are delivering their message. That physiology puts them in a state where they are transferring their energy across the phone. Even if they are not one-on-one with their prospects, they are delivering their energy across the phone because they are in that state of physiology.

So we always think of Physiology first: How is my state? How am I carrying myself? Where is my focus? On a day-to-day, am I more focused on problems or solutions? And we all know these people who believe that everything is wrong. You talk to them and they probably had a bad time at the grocery store and they couldn't find a parking spot, and the line was way too long, and the store was out of carrots, and the ice cream melted before they got home, and they hit a pothole, and the traffic was terrible, and the screen door at the

36

front of their house was broken… It never ends. A mentor of mine talks about data, not drama. How much drama do we carry around in our life? Here's the truth: Winners don't focus on drama. Winners never talk about problems. If they are talking about problems, they are talking about solutions. We don't talk about problems unless we talk about how to solve them. I will bring up problems because I want to solve them. I am bringing up problems because I want to figure out how to solve bigger and bladder problems. I am always working on solutions. When I am talking to my team, it's about what we are doing now that is working, what we should be doing, and what we are not doing now at all that we should be doing. I want feedback so that we can fix problems within our organization. Because you are a great leader and I'm a great leader, and I want to create more great leaders. So I'm looking for solutions to things that we haven't even thought about. **Forget about being problem-focused with the drama because I want to be solution-focused with the problem**. It's a slight slip but that is where the focus is. And where the focus goes, the energy flows.

So when we start to find ourselves constantly focused on the problem, what do we get more of? Problems. This takes into focus and language. Our language has to change for our outcome to change. And I want to talk about the language that is both internal and external. When you ask someone how their day is going, you are going to hear people say things like they are getting by, struggling along, another day, another dollar, still above the dirt, and so on. Is that how you feel? Is that how you want to carry yourself? Because here is the deal: this is your *primary statement*. Are you the guy who's walking around constantly saying things like "Why me? Why this? Why next? Why does it always happen to me? You've got to be kidding me!" And it follows you around and around and drags you down that rabbit hole. "You gotta be kidding me" becomes your primary statement.

How about you switch it around? What was the lesson I learned? What was the lesson here? What was the lesson in that? What is the lesson that I should have been learning here? How can I grow from this? How can I become better from this? So inside and outside, we are controlled by our inner voice. Here's the secret about the inner voice: It's *you*. It's you talking to you. You have more conversations with yourself than anyone else, and you have more conversations with yourself than anyone else has with you.

We talk to ourselves all day long. And sometimes, that is why we consider ourselves psycho because we are talking to ourselves all the time. And that person is doing what? That person is rationalizing with us, telling us rational lies, and convincing us of things that we shouldn't be convinced of. Because we are giving that person or that inner voice the power to do so or allowing that voice to make decisions for us, or to change our minds when our mind was already made up.

The secret is that you have the power to *silence* the voice, but you also have the power to give the voice positive power. If we focus on negative impact statements or negative primary statements, then the negative results are going to be energy that continues to resonate in our inner voice. This is where affirmations come in. Affirmations alone are not going to fix this for you. You can repeat a thing to yourself a hundred times, and then you can leave the house and start talking to yourself about how stupid that affirmations exercise was that you just did. All of a sudden, we go right back to being negative.

So affirmations don't work unless you carry them throughout the day unless you believe what you just read out loud; and unless you convince your inner voice of what your purpose is and what your results need to be, what your outcomes are going to be, and what your destiny is. People fake it all the time for money. Don't we fake it all the time to get to the end goal of the commission or the paycheck? Sometimes, we are faking it as a result. That is called chasing. Whenever we find ourselves chasing, the idea is that we are probably faking our story or our state, or our internal language is not in alignment with what we want as the outcome. And we are faking it just to get to the paycheck. Because we think they want the money, but what they want to do is create an alignment where the story matches the outcome. And getting those two things in alignment creates happiness.

We touched upon this in the beginning when we are living our unique selves. When I am talking about whatever it is that makes me happy and I am getting paid for it. Now, the world is right! But when I have to pretend that I am a realtor and put on a suit and tie, and show people houses who I don't want to show houses to with a smile on my face and ask them "What do you think about this house which is the last place in the world that I want to be?" Guess what? I'm not in alignment with my true self, and I have to fake being who I am because I am doing it for a paycheck. Now, I'm not in alignment. And guess what my internal voice is saying to me? It's saying why I'm doing this for a paycheck because this isn't who I am or who I am meant to be. This isn't what I was put here for.

You're doubting internally and you're doubting externally. Your voice and confidence level and what we call transference; you will never have the clarity and confidence to be who you want to be because you are faking it by wearing a mask. And those things won't be in alignment. It will always, at some level, deteriorate or erode your confidence or your clarity. It will come across in some way, shape, or form: Either you won't know where you are going or why you want to get there, or you won't have the confidence factor and people won't be able to recognize that with you. How many times have you seen somebody who pretends to be somebody they are not and you can smell it on them? You can sniff it out instantly. They do a social media post and a video that you watch and you automatically tell yourself that they have no idea what they are talking about. That's the confidence thing, and they are missing the confidence because they don't have the clarity about what it is that they are even talking about, to begin with.

But when you put it in alignment together, when you are in alignment and you have clarity about where it is that you are headed with something, confidence is automatic. What does a good speech coach say to someone who says that they are afraid to go on stage? A good speech coach will tell them to do what they are already good at. What could you talk about for fifteen minutes if I gave you a microphone? Because then it's not a speech. If you are in love with something, you could talk about it for fifteen minutes regardless of what the crowd thinks; I guarantee it! You probably know more shit about that thing that you love than the average person, so that is what you talk about. **Because when you are on stage, you are not fearful of the audience. You are fearful of not knowing your message**.

This is what happens in the real world when our language is not in alignment with our results and our outcomes, the things that we want to create in life then we don't have confidence about it. So our State and our language and our story have to line up. These Four Ss have to line up.

## *Story – Your Identity*

This brings me to The Story. What is my identity? If I get on stage and I have great physiology and I'm focused, centered, and using the right positive words, but I'm talking about something that I know nothing about, what am I going to do? Crumble. I am not going to be able to last ten seconds on that stage. If you start asking me to talk about something that I know nothing about in front of five thousand people, what is going to happen? My confidence level is going to go down to zero immediately, so my story has to be in alignment with my state. Am I a victim or am I a victor? Am I confident, can I own my role?

My story is based on my current and my future. Where am I heading? What you are going to find is that the people who are depressed or in a scared state, or they are fearful or worried or don't know where they want to go, are living in a past story. They are living in what they were taught. They are unsure, focused on the past, believing that they are not good enough or smart enough or that they are not in good enough shape. They were always taught that needed to have the education to do a particular job. No one has ever taught them how to do this so they assume they are not capable, so they think they need more education and need to learn more before they take action. All these story things that maybe they read somewhere or they saw on a YouTube video are in the past. The past happened this morning, yesterday, last week, ten years ago; it's all past. But the cool piece about your story is that you get to redefine it every day. You could wake up tomorrow and be a completely different person. You are allowed to do that. That's the cool piece about being human: You can redefine your story just by deciding what it is you want to be. That is who you are, like it or not. And then trajectory happens and that's what you do. That's your new story, and all of a sudden people want to get involved with your story. Most people don't get that they have the opportunity to redefine their story, and they get to decide if they are going to be the victim or the victor.

*"Be the hero of your movie. If you are going to recreate your story, why not be the hero?"*

**Joe Rogan**

Why not look at yourself as the hero of your movie? Why not elevate the thought of yourself to be that person that's going to take you up to an amazing trajectory? That's going to end you up in a place that you didn't even think possible? It will be one of those movies that, when it ends, you're going to go "wow, I didn't see that coming!" You can be that person, so you get to decide. But unfortunately, a lot of people play the victim. And their internal language is using a lot of 'don't' words. "I don't have enough money, I wish I didn't have to live paycheck to paycheck, I wish I didn't worry about money, I wish I didn't have to be worried about all these things…" when they should have been focused on the positive to create that new story.

*"I have all this opportunity in front of me. I'm grateful for the people in my life. I can't believe the opportunity and the team that I have in front of me, and the people that are being drawn to me like a magnet."*

I was always pretty strong with my story. I like to redefine my story. I think that I play with my story a lot. One of the things that have helped me with the trajectory when I learned about this was knowing that I can mold my story. I have been saying this for years that I truly believe that if every six months you look in the mirror, you should not even recognize the person you were six months ago. I want to challenge myself for growth. Six months or a year from now I should be facing new challenges, hiring people I think are way out out of my league, and investing in businesses that make me super uncomfortable. A year after that, I should be looking back saying to myself "that was easy compared to what I'm onto now". If I am not having that type of experience every six to nine months I know I'm not pushing myself to the level I want. Ask yourself when is the last time you had that kind of self-reflection?

The takeaway is that every year I want to push myself, my tribe pushes me, I push them, and I want to be surrounded by a tribe of people that pushes each other. Every year we should be working on what *next* year's goal is.

My business partners and I had a goal this year to ten self-storage facilities at $20 million a piece. That's $200 million. Keep in mind that this is already a stretched goal because of $200 million in our first year in developing the business. And I'm the visionary, so it's my job to cast the vision. My job is to make people look at me and say that they hope they can keep up with me. But my partner walked into my office last week and said he wanted to talk to me. I have known him for thirty years and he has never said that to me. He told me had been thinking that multi-families were so saturated right then and we were starting to hear people talk about storage and talk about storage. Nobody was talking about storage a year back. He told me that he thought we had a three-year window to hit this thing hard. Okay, I said, I got it because we were doing $200 million in ten deals that year. But he said we needed to do *twenty* deals that year. So basically, he wanted to do $400 million, and he said there wasn't any reason we couldn't do it. We had the team, we had the people, we had the resources, we had the investors… so yeah, let's do twenty deals! That's when I was saying to myself that what does that push me to? What kind of uncomfortable limit does that push me to? What would my story have to say to be that guy? I have to work my way into that role.

It is the definition of multiplicity: I'm forcing myself to multiply my state, my story, my strategy, and my standards to catch up with the person that I am trying to become. I have to get to that level so I need a different state, a different level of physiology, a different level of focus, a different level of language. I can't talk to myself like I am talking to myself right now. I have to talk to myself in different numbers. I have to talk to myself in different terms. My story cannot be the same and I cannot be the person who does ten deals in a year. Now I have to be the person who is going to do twenty deals in a year. I'm the leader who is leading twenty-five people, not twelve people. I'm the leader who has to coach people who are making $800,000 to $1,000,000 a year. I need people in my team who are doing that, so now I have to be the person who is recruiting them. I have to be the guy who has the balls to recruit them. So now, everything about me has to be different. And I was just getting comfortable with being a ten-deal guy. That's the whole point, and my partner just shakes it up and tells me to drop that skin that I'm wearing and get into this one. It's time to get to that next level. I didn't even think it was time for that yet, but we decided to graduate. It's at the exact moment you make the decision to make that shift into your new story we call this a **Paradigm Shift**. It's an almost visceral feeling when you feel it wash over you. You move into the new person, in this new dimension, that you've just taken ownership over; the next level of leadership.

The thing about great leaders creating great leaders is that it sounds like a cocky and condescending thing to say, but I am not talking about myself. It's the opposite. You pour into these guys to start with. I show them everything that I know, and then it becomes synergetic. Now, he's a great leader and he's throwing it right back on me, telling me to step up. He's helping me to create my Paradigm shift, lifting me up. And then I start to think to myself that how many guys like that does Jeff Bezos have who tell him to not just play small ball every time he walks into the office daily? How many people were there to push Jeff from just selling books online before he eventually took over a considerable chunk of all US retail sales direct to our front door? That's the difference, and when you have those types of leaders in your team, it is rocket fuel, it is game over. But until you breathe life into people like that, until you add trust and responsibility and accountability, none of that occurs.

## *Strategy*

Strategy is so many basic things, but it boils down to what your routines and rituals are. How you do one thing is how you do everything. It carries around my life. How clean is my truck? What does my desk look like? Do I make my bed in the morning? One of the best videos that you can watch is a naval officer saying, "If you want to change the world, make your bed." It starts with your routines and rituals, and one of them that I like to have is what I like to call "3 to thrive."

What does "3 to thrive" mean? It means that I want to knock down the three biggest things that are going to move the needle for me every single day. Throw out your list of thirty-five to-do items because they are horseshit. Nobody has thirty-five things to do each day that are going to move the needle for them. They probably have the top three things that are going to move the needle for them, but they get buried in their lists of things to do. Those are the top three difficult, disciplined, responsible things that you have to do, but what happens? They get pushed day to day to day while you do the other thirty-two bullshit, busywork, easy task that have nothing to do with your outcome. We come up with crap to do, we make stuff up to make ourselves feel good, but then we never do the high-gain, high-income activities that need to get done to move the needle for us.

So every day, try to pick 3 to thrive, three things that are going to change the game for us. These are what we call Gold Level Activities, and if they are in alignment with the outcome I seek. Once I know how to decide what my high-level goals are and how to knock them out of the park, are they on my calendar? Am I doing them every day? What are the top three things that I need to do to achieve my outcomes?

## *Standards*

Even though shit happens to me, I am not going to be defeated. Are you going to cry in your soup whenever you get a bad contract or a bad day or if somebody yells at you or you're on a sales call and they say no? Or, are you going to keep racking up those nos till you get a yes? How are you going to overcome the obstacles in your way? How are you going to pivot when the time comes? How are you going to hold yourself accountable every day? The answer is how you are showing up in everything that you do. How you are showing up to meetings, whether you are prepared or reacting. How you are showing up in one-on-one time with your team. Are you set up for that meeting with an agenda and come ready to go, or are you sloppy and a mess? Do you not know what you are doing, do you show up five minutes late for everything? We all know that person on our team that is known for being ten minutes late in everything. The people who play below the line and have poor standards for themselves have it all in alignment with a shit strategy. They always have a story and a lot of times it is related to their past. Their internal and external language is crap, always full of excuses for being ten minutes late, for having a flat tire, for having a crap car… it is always a story with drama. So when you find that people's Four Ss are not playing above the line or not doing what they need to do, it's usually because they are not playing up to their true potential.

Standards can also go as deep as your core values, your culture, how you control the way you look, the way you want to be perceived, the way you show up in physical form. Having joy, having a smile on your face. Joy is being happy and telling your face about it so that the people that you meet instantly like you because you seem so happy-go-lucky. So I have to remind myself to smile sometimes because I don't remember to smile, but it doesn't mean that I'm not happy. What are your standards for yourself? Sometimes I have to do the work and be disciplined about the standards that I want to set for myself. Because I want to pay attention to how I want to be perceived by my team. For a long time, I was a real asshole to my team, and I mean a real asshole. I would say whatever I felt like whenever I felt like it with no filter at the exact second. If somebody set me off, I would just snap. I have a story from years ago when I walked out of my office one day ultra-pissed at something, and I screamed out loud that I was going to fire everybody. This is back when I had maybe thirty-five employees in the office, and I don't even remember why I was so pissed off. And I remember that one of my executive assistants pulled me aside and she told me that I couldn't say all that stuff. I brushed it off saying that it was all in jest, but she was stern. She made me realize that the employees didn't know that I was kidding. Do you think that the $15/hour processor knows that the CEO is kidding when he runs around screaming, that he's going to fire everyone? That girl went home crying herself to sleep that night looking for a job. She didn't know I was kidding.

I'm a different human being now. But sometimes, I will do a meeting and I will say something where I mean well but someone will still point out that I was a little hard on someone. Even my well-meaning advice can come off harsh. Okay, I guess that means I will have to smile the next time I give someone advice about a sales call. I assume that people have thick skin but while I don't have any ill-will in my calls anymore, back then I meant meanness. I was a total asshole back then.

So as a leader, how are you perceived by your people? What do you want for your people? I want to love my people, I do love my people and I want to be surrounded by people who I love legitimately. People do not work for me that I don't like anymore, and people don't believe me when I say that. They will say that it is impossible to have a whole team full of people that you love. Bullshit, and I will fight you on that. If you are on my team and I don't sincerely think that you are a rock star, you will not stay. It will not happen because I will set a set of expectations for you that you agree to that you will not be able to keep up with, and that is okay. I will tell to your face with crystal-clear clarity – because I have done this so many times – that if you cannot meet these expectations that we agreed to, then this might not be the place for you. Also, you are probably not meeting those expectations because your passion is somewhere else. And that is okay, I will help you find a seat in someone else's company where you belong where you will be happier.

Because if you are not happy here and not meeting your expectations and not passionate about jumping out of bed and coming to work here, then I don't want you and you don't want to be here. So why are we dating? Why are we in this relationship? I am too old for this shit. I don't want to be in a relationship with someone who doesn't want me; I am old enough to admit that. So there is no reason for us to be in it. I used to have fifty people in a relationship that I didn't want to be in. Imagine that! I do not want that ever again. If you are in a relationship that you don't want to be in, you are faking it, which means that your energy and time are being wasted on shit that doesn't produce anything. And if that isn't bad enough in a physical relationship when you are dating someone, imagine when there is money involved. Imagine when every Friday you are cutting a check to someone who you don't like. That is resentment. You feel like you can't stand this person and yet you pay them to be there. Nothing eats you like that. Inevitably, you end up firing them and you pay them for unemployment forever.

And then that horrible person you didn't like stays on unemployment forever because they were lazy, to begin with, so they won't even go and get a new job. They will just stay on unemployment and you end up paying them forever, so they become cancerous to you. I mean psychologically, energy level-wise, the whole thing. So just cut the loss. I found out the hard, hard way to build a team just by finding the people you love to be around.

# Chapter 3

# Plan of Execution

---

**#5 Multiplicity is ACTION; Intelligent and Inspired Action daily towards a worthy outcome.**

Believe it or not, more people spend time planning their vacation to Mexico for a week than they do planning out their life. They know the plane that they are going to fly on, what date they are taking off on, when they are going to land, where they are going to sit, what hotel they are staying in, whether it has a courtyard view or an ocean view, what temperature it is going to be when they get there, what they're going to pack, what they're going to eat, reservations, they know it all down to a T!

But try and ask somebody what their goals are for this quarter? What do they want to accomplish? What relationships do they want to build? What kind of people do they hope to meet this quarter? What do they want to do for their team? What would be the results and the purpose of growing those people to another level?

Are they not thinking about this because a whole year is such a big window of time or is it because it is something that is out of control of their lives? Answer: Both. In this place or this stage, they don't think that they are attached to a story where they set goals every year and they don't get achieved, plain and simple. So why even bother setting them? Or maybe they haven't been taught how to put together a good plan and execute it.

*"This isn't the stuff that is taught in schools. Schools don't even teach you how to balance a checkbook, so they certainly aren't going to teach you how to create a business plan or, if they do, you were probably asleep when they did anyway."*

When Seabees go overseas, we have to know what we're doing when we get there before we deploy. I have to understand what I'm building, what materials and tools are needed, who is coming with me, and what my plan of attack will be.

We just aren't paying attention to this stuff because it isn't important when you are a kid, but it is important now. But as adults, we don't work on it or pay attention to it. It's just this one-week window that does nothing except give you some type of enjoyment, but they aren't planning the next fifty-one weeks out of the year about where they want to be the next month or the next year, or how they are going to get more money or be freer. Because they are only thinking about this short window which in itself is probably society, but also that limiting belief of being in control of this one week so they can just focus on this.

*"Let's get crystal clear on this plan of execution: We want to know exactly where we are today and exactly where you want to go. And above all else, how we can close the gap between those two. That's the plan, and the whole goal is to turn decades into days. It's called compressing time."*

The reality of it is that the reason that it takes us so long to do things is that we don't execute on them or a plan. We wallow around the Earth and think that one day it will get done, but it never does. And then we look back on our deathbed and regret not doing all the things we wanted to do. The only difference between the person who gets it done and the person who doesn't is a plan, an executable plan. But what is preventing you from taking the first steps? What is it that is blocking you, what is the obstacle, the hang-up? What is it that is keeping you from moving forward? Because you have sure as heck planned out your vacation in Mexico! You didn't just whip out your AMEX and say that I'm going, so take me away!

No, you figured and planned all that out. So why don't you do the same for your life? Oftentimes, people feel like the limiting factor is bigger and bolder than it is. In other words, they think that whatever is blocking them or holding them back is bigger than it is until they take a couple of minutes and think about it. Once that is out of the way, they're likely to realize that it wasn't such a big deal after all. All they had to do was write it down or take thirty quiet minutes and spend some time thinking about this. We call that taking intelligent and inspired action towards the outcome. It's like going up a flight of steps: You take the first couple of steps and get going, and then you see the next couple of steps and start jumping steps or moving faster. It's the same thing with taking that first initial step. That is all it takes to get going to become outcome-focused.

*"Being outcome-focused is where you know your destination, you know why you want to get there, and you know what you want to get out of it. That is having an actual plan of action and execution."*

# Chapter 4

# Checking Your Toolkit

Once we get rid of limiting beliefs in step one, and then we create a roadmap or a plan of action or the recipe in step two, we then move on to step three which I call Checking Your Toolkit. I use this analogy a lot from the Seabees because that is where I come from, that if I wanted to deploy and had a Jobsite and knew my materials on hand, knew where I had to build, the manpower I needed, basically exactly what I needed for the job, I would also deploy with a toolkit. And by this, I mean a literal toolkit, or a box of tools if you will. Back in the day, we didn't have any fancy power tools at all, we would have hand tools and saws and screwdrivers, stuff like that. Here's the truth: You can get rid of your limiting beliefs and can have an incredible plan of attack, but if you don't have sustainable practices, daily habits, routines, rituals, and those things that create systems and support to your outcome, none of the above is going to come together. These are your tools. So what I do is, walk people through an exercise and ask them what kind of tools they have at their disposal. What resources they are not utilizing to 100% of their capacity or potential.

*"Truthfully, it is never a matter of your resources, but it is a matter of your resourcefulness, which I'm sure you've heard a lot. We want to check the toolkit and figure out what we need for the job ahead, but a lot of the toolkit is right between your two ears. We want to make sure that we are mentally prepared and then have the tools for the job ahead."*

The systems for support are about the people around you, the rituals, and daily habits, and so on. It's what you put in your body and what you put in your mind. It is everything sustainable. It is these things that you can do and want to do forever. What you find then is that people fall into these two categories. The first are those who create systems and don't sustain them. People can have an amazing CRM that does everything they need to do but they just won't learn how to do it so they don't sustain the practice.

That's the problem because we chase this shiny object that we're looking for, this push-button solution for overnight millions. I want a CRM that I never have to log into and just does it all for me so that my sales simply start rolling in while I lay on my couch and watch Netflix. That's one category of people. The second category includes those people who create these great systems and it is like a New Year's Resolution. They just disappear and fall off. I've created this amazing impactful system that works for me and it makes sense but, just like a New Year's Resolution or how going to a gym makes sense, they are hard to do. I don't want to do the work, so then they get lazy, and it just disappears. Therefore we have to make sure that we create systems, structures, and support that you are going to be able to utilize. Sometimes it takes work, but sometimes it just takes creating the right systems that are going to support you as well.

So take an internal ToolKit audit of your own: What systems, resources, relationships, team members, software, equipment, etc. do you have that:

- You are not utilizing 100% efficiency
- You are not using it at all (and maybe paying for it)
- Should be using but don't make the time
- Don't need anymore

So many of us are "chasing" shiny objects or the next best thing to make us wealthy overnight when the answer to our problems is creating efficiencies and becoming resourceful with the tools we have right in front of us.

I've built buildings with hand tools and I've made over $100k a month with a pen, notepad, and a cell phone. Trust me, you can too. It's not in the software, widget, or bot.

# Chapter 5

# Controlling The Clock

---

**Multiplicity is CONTROLLING the CLOCK; Executing Daily, High Gain Activities at Home, High-Income Activities at work.**

Probably the most impactful of all the five things that we are discussing here is what I call the Rule of 168. If you're not familiar with it, we all have a hundred and sixty-eight hours a week to live out our life. There is not a single person on Earth who has more than a hundred and sixty-eight hours, except for maybe Elon Musk because he's an alien. We have to eat, sleep, pay our bills, play with our kids, and have our playtime by going to the gym. But what are you going to do with the rest of your time? A hundred and sixty-eight is all you have each week, so what I want to do is figure out a way to allot time for what I call high impact and high-income activities. Taking care of your family, taking care of your body, reading, listening to great podcasts, listening to audible books, growing as a leader, becoming a better coach, and thinking about ways that you can create opportunities for your team. So how are we creating high-income activities and how are they making it onto our calendar so that we execute on them?

What we do is that we take out time to check in to what I call a time management audit, where we figure out the areas where we are playing below the line and how we need to change that to start playing above the line. Inside of that time management audit come the Four Ds: We should either Do It, Delay Doing It, Delegate It, or just Dump It altogether. Within those Four Ds, we want to maximize our time because it is a matter of what we do with our time that makes us different.

On the Do side, I always classify this as if you can do it in five to ten minutes and you have the free time to do it, *do* it. I want to eliminate something called decision fatigue at all costs, meaning that so many of us are carrying this weight of decisions on our plate. If someone asks you to do something, say that you'll get back to them. If someone sends you an email and it gets stuck in your inbox, you have to respond to it. Simple tasks and responses where what happens is that it starts to weigh on us as human beings. It's becoming nothing more than mental junk, and whether or not you are consciously thinking about it, your subconscious on the other hand is still thinking about it.

*"This is the hard thing that most people have to understand: Your brain is being clogged up by this junk regardless of whether or not you proactively want it to be. You have to eliminate decision fatigue."*

So when somebody asks you to do something or asks for your time, and it is something you want to do, and it doesn't fall onto the other three Ds, just do it. I heard something great that "For those of you having a hard time making decisions, flip a coin. And while it's in the air, you'll know what decision you are wishing for before it hits your hand." So just go with the gut.

*"Too many of us try to rationalize or tell "rational lies" about why we should or shouldn't do something. You have already made the decision. Your brain decides in a microsecond, and your subconscious already did the math."*

As a leader, you need to trust your gut and be confident with yourself. This is a muscle that you can work on by learning to make quick decisions. Learn to live with your decisions, make them, execute them, and move forward. The biggest and baddest entrepreneurs that you know do not vacillate over things like whether or not they want a ham and cheese or a turkey and cheese; they just make a decision. If you ever ask me what I want for lunch, I'll simply tell you to get me what you get because I don't want to make a decision. I don't want that taking the precious time of my conscience, so I'll live with whatever it is you're eating.

Decision fatigue is so important. Stop second-guessing yourself and do it, because the more you learn to just do it, the better and more confident you get and you stop worrying about it. That's the best benefit of this. Your $10 decisions happen fast, then you're making $100 decisions fast, then you're making $10,000 decisions fast. Next thing you know, you're making $100,000 decisions fast because you learned to trust your instincts. It doesn't matter. I know it's a yes or no when you ask me the question. I don't second guess myself or rationalize whether or not I'm right or wrong. I don't need to. I already know the answer. That's the compression of time as every second you burn on this decision is time lost on something else. It's a mental weight like carrying around body armor.

*"It's not so much the fact that you want to make fast decisions; it's the fact that your brain already made the decision. That's the distinction that people need to understand."*

65

When I ask you if you like coffee or tea, you already know the answer. Now you say to yourself, "Do I like tea better? I'm not sure, I like tea sometimes." You already know you like coffee! It's over. When I ask you if you want a house in Newport Beach, CA, or a house in South Florida, you probably say, "Well, I'm not sure…" Yes, you are! You are already sure. You have made the decision already. They might both be amazing choices, but you have already decided. The point is that it's not so much a fast decision, it's a matter of your subconscious already deciding for you, and you don't want to wrestle with your subconscious. You want to give your subconscious the freedom to make choices because it is going to help you exercise that muscle and trust that muscle. Ultimately, that is going to give you more confidence as an entrepreneur, as an owner, and even as a person to start to make those decisions in life. Eventually, you're going to become better across the board because of it.

If you think about the Five Freedom once again, all of those are created when you control the clock. When you control Time Freedom, all the rest starts to relate with itself. When you start to control the outcome, all the rest of it starts to fall into play. But if you can't make decisions, how are you going to create freedom for yourself? This is probably one of the most impactful ones out of the Four Ds.

The second one is Delay Doing It, and the rule here is that if I delay it, it must be delayed properly. Meaning that it has to be delayed to my calendar, and that turns it into a task or a calendar invite, or something that is removed from my subconscious so that I don't have to think about it anymore. For example, let's say I have to get back to someone about something. If I leave it in my email inbox, I'll just keep staring at it every day every time I check my inbox say three to five times a day or if some people check their emails a hundred and fifty times a day even, they are going to see the person up there a hundred and fifty times a day. Once they do that, they will keep reminding themselves that they have to get back to the person a hundred and fifty times a day! No. Just take it and put it on a calendar. Three days from then, I'll be reminded that I have to get back to the person. Subconsciously, I don't have to think about it anymore till the due date.

Number three is Delegate It. Delegate It has its own set of rules. You have to delegate it to someone capable of and responsible for doing it. This is a big one for a lot of business owners and entrepreneurs, because how many times do you think they have delegated something to someone who is then incapable of doing it, and they end up doing it for them. Or they end up giving themselves an additional task of not just telling someone to do it but also teaching and training them how to do it. That is not delegating, folks! That is doubling your dysfunction. You have to delegate tasks to people you trust, and if you don't trust them then we're going to have to learn how to trust them. That is creating responsibility and accountability within your team by delegating. By the way, delegating is one of the best ways that you can lift your team by giving them responsibility and not micromanaging that responsibility.

Last but not the least, one of those things that some people – especially people pleasers – have a hard time doing, is Dump It. How many things on your list don't even need to happen? By the way, delaying and dumping are pretty well-related, because if you delay those fires that you put out for an hour or six hours or even a day, guess what happens when you circle back to them? They solve themselves! Now, you don't need to handle it. No doing, no delaying, no delegating. I don't need to interact with anyone over it because it's over. So I can just dump it by delaying it sometimes.

How many times do you feel like you have to jump or react to everything that hits your plate the *second* it hits your plate? Now, all of a sudden, I'm creating more chaos for myself. Very efficient people or high earners know whether they can just dump it right away. I can almost self-delegate to somebody who comes to me with a problem by saying that they can book a time to talk to me about the problem but you also need to bring three solutions. My people are trained to come to me with solutions because while I do want to hear about the problem, I am more interested in hearing the solutions. That is an automatic delegation as I want to hear your feedback about what is working and what isn't. But at the same time, I'm not here to solve your problem, I'm here to listen.

Warning*** Don't catch yourself being the kind of "leader" that solves everyone's problems for them. This is the opposite of Multiplicity. This is a disease that will trap you in a lifetime JOB. Your people will decide they can't be trusted to solve problems on their own. You will never get a day off again and all your hopes of time freedom will go out the door.

They need you to teach them to fish more than they need to watch your fish. The other voice is just your ego.

*"I don't pay you to bring me problems, I pay you to solve problems."*

# Chapter 6

# Execution and Accountability

We can have the mindset, we can have a great plan of action, we can have our toolkit in alignment and we can have everything controlled by the clock. But this is where it can all fall apart if we don't have it dialed in right, and that is a lack of execution. How many people do you know have analysis paralysis? They never take their first step or action, even though they know everything or have been to every mastermind, or read every book or invest in every course, and then never bought a house. They hadn't been executed because they were paralyzed. So we have to now execute, we have to now move forward. Take action on all the things that we have worked on so far, otherwise, why did we put all that effort in? Lack of execution is one of those killers.

## #2 Multiplicity is in MOTION; Playing above the line, Chasing the next Paradigm shift, Always Adapt and Evolve.

The next thing is a lack of course correction or being able to adapt and evolve. Oftentimes instead of execution, you find yourself chasing a to-do list or having busy days that never seem to move the needle. That is a lack of execution, so execution has to be done right and on the right things, not just putting out fires. A lack of execution can also be your goals just being ideas without a plan, or having a plan that you aren't executing daily in the alignment of your goals. How many people execute daily but their goals are completely misaligned with what they are supposed to be doing each day? Maybe you did a thing today or yesterday, but how many of those things are in alignment with your goals? None of them, because you're just doing your job. In that case, you're not going to stop chasing. That was *the chasing you*, and you chasing things was just doing things just for the sake of doing them not in alignment with your goals. That is execution without having a plan.

So lack of course correction is realizing what is going to happen when you have to pivot. Are you going to cry in your soup if something goes wrong, or are you going to shift and realize that it is an issue and decide on how to fix it to move forward? Think about pulling out of your driveway in the morning. The roads are not perfect; you're going to hit speed bumps, potholes, sometimes it is going to snow or rain. But it doesn't mean you don't drive the car or not go to your job or drop your kids off at school. You will just have to drive differently to course-correct, and get resourceful when things don't go your way. Adapt! So many people have a plan and start executing, but when shit doesn't go their way they just clam up and stop. They say this isn't how they worked it out, or this isn't what they said it would be like. "Joe told me it was all going to work out this way, but it didn't. That's it, I'm done. I quit!" This takes us right back to the mindset when we tell ourselves rational lies about why we're not good enough for this or cut out for this. We even tell ourselves that maybe we shouldn't even try. If we failed once, why try again? Why don't I just go back to my 9-to-5?

*"Course correction is an evolution that never stops. This is where a lot of people fall short because they don't realize that everyone you have ever looked up to, from the biggest to the baddest, is course-correcting daily, and they are making bigger mistakes daily than you have ever dreamed of because they want to get to a level of goal that you have never dreamed of. They have to make those mistakes to get there."*

Last but not least in this trifecta is accountability. How are you measuring up? How are you tracking it? Who is holding you accountable? And wouldn't it make sense to have someone co-create with you and hold you accountable? If you are accountable to a partner who is not a mentor or a coach, or preferably a partner who is somebody you pay and pay to be invested with, how are you accountable to them? I go to the gym at 5 a.m. A lot of people tell me that I'm nuts. I live in the North East and it is cold there. If my gym buddy was my accountability partner, I would just text him at 4:15 am about how freaking cold it is and that I am sleeping in today, he would be totally on board with that.

But if I am paying $75 an hour to an ex-pro IFBB trainer to meet me at the gym at 5 a.m., he would just look at my text and tell me to get my ass out of the bed or he will come over and break my legs. He is showered and ready to walk out the door by the time 4:15 am rolls around, and will not rest till I get my money's worth. That is accountability because I know what I need to do and he knows what I need to do. Whether I want to do it or not, I *have* to do it because that this what is going to make me successful. That is what is going to put me in alignment with my goals. Therefore I want an accountability partner who is going to keep me on track and co-create with me along the way on the days that I want to and on the days I especially don't want to. Having accountability is the paramount key to all these five steps.

73

We rationalize why we do or don't need accountability by telling ourselves that if we have a business, my business partner is going to be my accountability partner. But your partner is in it with you together, and if you have a shitty week, they have a shitty week and you're both commiserating together. Who is holding you accountable?

*"'Oh, we both screwed up. Let's chalk it up and do it again next week.' That is not accountability, it is co-misery. That is not holding you accountable to do something but both of you being in alignment to screw it up."*

Therefore, it has to be someone on the outside that wants to root for you and see you grow but is also responsible enough to know what you need even when you don't know what you need. That is why great coaches are great coaches. Don't get me wrong, there are a million shitty coaches packed on social media right now, but the fact is that a great coach is going to accelerate you a thousand times more than you pay them. I don't care what they charge; if they are holding you accountable to do what you do and your goals are high enough, you hire a coach. Especially if you are a top achiever who wants to see extraordinary success.

One of the biggest challenges is that in business, in life, in planning in general – I have gone through five hundred different variations of planning, goal setting, goal achievement, the goal this and goal that. I have written out the full-length twenty-page business plan of what your SWOT analysis is, what your challenges are, what your end-revenue goals are, how you are going to build your team. And this, the COI and the RPM, is the simplest, quickest, most productive way that I have ever found to line up your goals and knock them out of the park in the shortest period. It gets to the meat and potatoes quicker than anything that I have ever done. We call it the Seven Simple Steps for that reason. It is the art and science of goal setting and goal achievement, and it breaks it down to the simplest form. It is two parts: The COI which is the **Centers for Improvement**, and the RPM which is the **Rapid Planning Method**.

With COIs, I like to start with ten COIs, list ten things. The important part about these ten things is that I break them out into five and five. Most people focus on business: Revenue, revenue, and revenue! Therefore the first five COIs are personal. What five things do I want to improve in my personal life, and then take five quiet minutes to think about those five things. They might be fitness, my finances, travel planning, getting clarity on my calendar considering I have no idea how to use the damn thing. They might be that I want to spend more quality time with my kids and my wife. They might be that I want to have a better relationship with my spouse or my significant other. They might be a myriad of different things. They might even be spending more time on my hobbies. Some people have hobbies that they just don't mess with. Maybe it's time that they start getting back in touch with the things that make me happy. Ultimately, the top five personal things  – and this is the secret sauce – are the things that are going to help you move the needle with the business things.  The kid-like mentality, the dreams; all of that are going to push you with the fuel and energy that you need. And what do we do? We focus directly on the professional stuff until we burn out and we go back to the chasing. We are chasing, chasing, chasing, and then we never catch anything. But worst of all, we never enjoy the ride. Because ultimately, that is what we are here for To enjoy the ride. There is no secret endgame, we just need to figure out the Five Freedoms along with the ride.

This brings us to the bottom five COIs. Now, these might look professional, they might look like I want to get involved in some coaching or some mentorship and I want to personally develop my business skills. They might look like I want to grow a particular department or I want to learn how to become a better recruiter. Or I want to write a book. How are you going to move the needle on your business side? Maybe you want to develop a better marketing plan. Whatever that strategy looks like, just come up with five items and give it the quiet mental time to journal it and write it down. Here's the fun part:

After you come up with these ten items, the next thing you want to do is *gamify* them. You want to gamify it by coming up with sexy, cool, compelling, interesting names for these things. Now, these are personal things to you. You are not going to be sharing these with anybody, no one is going to ask you to put these on the internet or Facebook and hold yourself accountable by telling the world that you want to increase your sex life with your wife and you're calling it kinky time. No one is going to put this out there. This is for you to remember and it creates a psychological link because it is gamified. Maybe your hobby is working on your past project, and you have a nickname for it. That's how you are going to gamify it and you are going to create a link psychologically to the nickname of the COI. It makes it fun, it makes it interesting, and ultimately, what you are going to do is that you are going to map these things out so that they are going to make it on your calendar.

So you will look forward to spending time working or gamifying this time on your hobby or your business thing. Even if it is a professional COI, you can gamify it with a fun title around. That way you can look forward to doing it at two o'clock in the afternoon for ninety minutes. You will be improving that category of your life, whether it is personal or business. So gamify it with a juicy title, something that you are interested in that only matters to you. That is phase one.

Phase two is what we call RPMs. There are Seven Simple Steps to setting goals and knocking them out of the park. What I want to instill in people is that these are simple steps. These are not meant to be utterly complicated or things that you are going to create a book report on. These are things that I want you to practice with quickness and speed, and I want ultimately you to be able to re-teach to anyone around you so that they start to do it quickly. You don't want to get lost in here, so when you do this exercise for the first time, I want you to just pick one, just one COI, and just go through it. And I want you to go through it relatively quickly. You are going to start with the result that you are looking to achieve. Let's say that the result is working on your hobby, and if your hobby is being an automobile enthusiast, then your result and your outcome are that you are going to finally fulfill your dream of getting your current car project out on the road. Remember that you are always focused on the outcome. That's the impact, that is what is going to happen. You are going to feel yourself behind the wheel. Paint a picture of the result you are looking towards, and if the result is a business purpose then it is maybe that you are building your marketing plan. The result and outcome here are that you are going to have automatic calls and leads coming in every day of the week for your team to be able to go out there and close. Whatever the result and outcome are, you are going to state it in step one. It could be through a combination of direct mail or pay-per-click advertising, but you will make your outcome happen.

So that is step one: The Result. That is the R in RPM. Step two is Purpose. What is the purpose behind you doing this? The purpose for an auto enthusiast, to take our previous example, is to feel at their best. When does that happen? When they are driving down the highway in their latest car project with the windows down and the rumble of the engine. They feel at their best when they are reminiscing about being a child again because that is the last time they were in that car that they just restored. You could say they had a moral obligation to put it together so that they can feel more complete because it had been gnawing at them for a long time. That is a purpose statement, and once they are done, they are going to feel a lot better about themselves. It completes a piece of them.

I should asterisk the R and the P here because this is what happens every time with RPMs. We want to avoid this stuff because this is the emotional, sticky, icky, have to think about and have to put actual effort into, what is the result and purpose and so on, and you don't want to do this stuff because this is what you have to think about. Meanwhile, you want to jump into the next step, which is called the MAPs section. That is the Massive Action Plan, which is where you are going to brain dump. Think about when you were a kid in elementary school and your teacher told you to start writing whatever is on your mind, just start blowing it out there and it doesn't matter what happens.

Whatever silly story happens is kind of like a brain dump that you are going to just drop on the paper and we would edit it later because your creativity will come out. This is kind of a brain dump. I want you to think about all the things that need to happen to create the outcome that you need. So if it is a car project, it might be getting a parts list together, having the metal inspected to see if there is any rust that needs to be repaired, setting up a body guy, ordering a new set of wheels, getting the interior looked at, tuning the motor, ordering a muffler... what is the list of the things that need to happen? What is the Massive Action Plan that needs to go into creating the result that you are looking for?

If we're talking about reflecting on a marketing plan, it might be finding a pay-per-click guy, finding a direct mail resource, putting up a post on social media, looking for someone who knows a good pay-per-click guy, talking to your team about how much volume needs to be sent and how many leads on average they want to get back in so they aren't overwhelmed, making sure you have the linkage set up so that when the calls come in then they are going to the right phone numbers and they are connecting properly. It might be putting together a little bit of a sales flow so that the team knows where the leads are coming into. This way they know that they are coming from pay-per-clicks so they can use a different script for it, and maybe you have to write the script. It is one big brain dump of all the stuff that will become your Massive Action Plan.

This is what happens when people start to set goals up: They jump right to the MAPs. If you say to someone that you need a marketing plan, what do they do? They jump right to the MAPs. But they forgot the first two, the Result and the Purpose, and without those two everything else feels empty. It makes a big difference because, without them, you are not tied to an outcome. You are tied to a list of tasks. If I ask you why is it so important for you to have this marketing plan together, what is your answer? Because you have all these tasks that you need to do, so you're busy. But if you answer that your result and outcome have to be the fulfillment of your team thanks to having the lead flow that they need so that they can close the deals they need to close to make the money they need to make to feed their families. And what is your purpose is? Your purpose is that you feel your best when you become the leader that you need to become to create this output for your team and show them that you and your team are capable together to create the lead flow they need to perform at their maximum output. That is your purpose for doing this. It is why you have to step out of the box to become the person you need to become. Remember, it always goes back to how I do one thing is how I do everything. If you half-ass this RPM, you will get half-assed results. Take ten minutes and do this and I promise you that it will take you just ten minutes. That is all it takes. The problem is that we don't have the bandwidth or we think that we don't do this, so we like to skip ahead. It is so impactful, so important to do the R and the P.

Now that we have the Massive Action Plan which is step three, we take it to step four which is Prioritization. This is where we come up with our 3 to thrive, where you want to go back to your MAPs and pick out the top three things you listed in your brain dump that are going to move the needle. What are the first three things that you have to do, or maybe the first three things that, if you did them, would make the rest of the things irrelevant? Maybe if you delegate your PPC to somebody else, the next thing you know is that your marketing plan is done. Or if you do these three things, your needle moves way off to the right. The thing is 90% complete.

Number five is called Time Stamping. What gets scheduled, gets done. Number five is where I am going to take those 3 to thrive, and I am going to drag them into my calendar. Forty-five to ninety-minute increments, depending on how long they may take to do, I'm going to time block those three items. Some of them might be fifteen-minute items like sending an email, posting something on social media, whatever they might be. But the reality of it is that they have to hit your task list or your calendar. They have to become part of your calendar. They have to live somewhere or, you might have guessed it, they won't get done.

Number six is Leverage. This is when we ask ourselves who can get us there to the desired result that we seek. Who do I need to hire? Who do I need to delegate this to? Is there someone already on my existing team or is there a professional who can do this for me? Maybe there is a third-party service that can do this for me or help me get there quicker. Or maybe it is a friend who is in my tribe who can help me in marketing. Who do I know that can help me launch this thing quicker than if I did it all by myself?

*"Leverage your tribe, leverage your resources, leverage your leaders."*

Last but not least is number seven: Execution and Course Correction. Now that it is on your calendar, you have to do it. When you start to execute those 3 to thrive and you hit a roadblock, what happens? Will, you just say fuck it, you're not doing it? That there is no reason to work on this Center of Improvement because you just hit a roadblock? No, you have to go back to your MAPs and see if you can adjust them or cross it out, whatever it is you need to do. Because at the end of the day, your result and your purpose have not changed. You cannot stop doing this until you are done. When you create the outcome, you have to go get the outcome. If my team wants me to do twenty deals this year, you have to get that outcome. That is your result. That is your purpose.

Now, you have to Course Correct till you reach that outcome, and when you do, you can go back to your COI list and scratch that sucker off so that you can feel free to add more on if you want. But the beauty of these working ten items is if you keep that list going, you can update it. You check something off, you put something back on it thanks to the open spot.

It is also important to realize that this is not a time-defined thing. There are things that you put on there that you can do in a week, or there are things you put in there that might take a year. There is no pressure to do these things. The only pressure is that you need to push the needle every week. So you can look at some personal stuff, you can look at some business stuff. Some weeks you are going to spend more time on personal stuff, some weeks you are going to spend more on business stuff. It is up to you, but what you want to do is make sure that you're putting 3 to thrive on your calendar every day. And it might be one thing from this item or two things from that item. But here's the thing: On a Sunday afternoon, you can very easily look at your ten items and each one of them has 3 to thrive, you can just plug them into your calendar throughout the week. Now you know that every day you are doing three things that are going to move you closer to the outcome that you seek.

*"Ask yourself this: How often are you doing three things each day that are getting you closer to an outcome that you seek to improve one of the things in your personal, or one of the things in your business life? If it gets on your calendar, it gets done."*

One of the most important things to understand here is that if you want to create time freedom, time freedom is not being free of time or being free of a clock. Time freedom is *controlling* the clock. It's an opposite mindset. People think that sitting on the beach is time freedom, but controlling the clock to where you can sit on the beach is time freedom. Last year this time, I was in St. Thomas on the beach at the DM family retreat for five days. I would get up at 5 am, do my morning routine, work out, take the kids to breakfast, do my mastermind calls in the morning, go spend three hours with the DM family in the conference room, go have lunch, go to the beach for three hours, schedule a call at 4 o'clock, go to dinner with the family, and then have whatever I had in the evening. So it's blocking time to have freedom.

That's the difference. You don't just say fuck it and throw your clock and calendar out of the window and start drinking. That is not a time freedom thing. I'm a jet skier and I just bought two new jet skis. I and my business partner love it, that's our thing. But guess what? You don't go down the shore in New Jersey on Saturday and Sunday with a jet ski because it is freaking suicide. There are like ten million people there. So what do I do? On Thursday afternoon, I get in the car and head down to the shore, and I will jet ski every Thursday during the summer. And I can do that because I have time freedom. I get up Thursday morning, do my mastermind call with my team from 9:45 to 10:45 in the morning, then I will get in my truck, drive down to the shore, get on my jet ski, go bar-hopping for the rest of the afternoon, get back in my car at 4 o'clock, drive home and have dinner with my family. That is time freedom.

In between bar-hopping, I will check my email probably two or three times, but I won't be tied to my phone all day long. I won't be on my phone all day calling people because I have to. That time is blocked: Nobody can book appointments with me or schedule discovery calls or coaching or pick my brain. That shit doesn't happen during jet ski time because it is time blocked, just like it doesn't happen during family dinner time. It's controlling the clock. When you block the time, the time is blocked, and I am doing stuff in that time.

# Chapter 7

# Multiplicity by Gratitude

---

**#4 Multiplicity is MINDSET; Attitude of Gratitude and Focused on a Bigger Tomorrow.**

*"When you're feeling helpless, get helpful."*

Multiplicity by gratitude is just getting out of the funk. In other words, it is about creating rocket fuel when you are in the dumps. We all have these days where we are down and out for a day that turns into a week and a month, and a lot of people are having this issue particularly with the pandemic lockdown of 2020. So how do we course correct in an instant?

Knowing when it is happening, knowing when it is coming, and what things can jump us out of it.

The law of polarity states that where it is hot, there must also be cold. Vice versa, where there is cold, there must be hot. You wouldn't know what hot is without cold. If you never experience hot, then you wouldn't know what cold was. If you never experience dark, then you wouldn't know that it was light outside right now. These are the reverse forces of nature. The same thing with the North Pole and the South Pole, we wouldn't have the North Pole if there wasn't the South Pole. So the law of polarity states that opposites need to exist for us to feel the difference or understand the difference. This is the same with pleasure and pain: You wouldn't know pleasure unless you experienced pain. You wouldn't know what it's like to create a big win unless you went through a shit-ton of losses.

*"Everybody wants easy overnight success."*

Ultimately, the problem is that in today's generation, we are going towards this push-button millions mentality. They want to invest $5 and make $5,000 without doing anything for it. They do not want to hire someone and get help, or engage with anybody or build relationships, or get to know people, and they certainly don't want to add value. All this stuff that are buzzwords that sell people into a thing is the opposite of what people want to hear. You hear people say, "sell them what they want and give them what they need." This is the problem with society. I have to sell you on picking up my book to make a billion dollars. And then I have to give you this, "okay, you lazy shit. You have to work! That's how you make a billion dollars." And you'll be all amazed because this is what you need. You need to experience pain to understand pleasure. You need to execute, adapt, evolve, and hit the freaking potholes.

*"You need to be punched in the face a lot to grow."*

People think that these entrepreneurs have it together. Take Elon Musk for example. The reality of it is that he is the wealthiest guy on the planet, and he is broke all the time! No one talks about how he sells PayPal and takes the entire investment to buy another company while he is living in his apartment and can't pay his rent. It is freaking fantastic, but it is also probably the biggest expanse of the law of polarity that you have ever seen. It is also why he can create the vision and the traction behind why he is who he is.

Amazing visionaries paint a picture and cast an image and people want to follow that because of the law of polarity. They can create and cast that image because they know that they have been in Shitsville, have done all the work, and know what the top of the mountain looks like because they have been under it and fought for it.

I use Conor McGregor as an example a lot because he is one of the most prolific fighters ever, and he has been knocked out, choked out, had his ass kicked. I can remember his losses more than his wins. Of course, he has more wins than losses, but he gets his ass kicked a lot. He is still the most popular fighter and is the most well-paid fighter. He is not afraid to get in the ring and get his block knocked off. He is cool with it because he knows that when he gets his block knocked off, it's going to teach him how to experience more pleasure. He's going to go in there and – win or lose – he's going to learn, and he's going to earn. He's going to leave that ring and make $25 million whether he wins or loses, it doesn't matter. And he is willing to put himself out there because of that.

Most people just want to go in and experience bliss, but they don't want to get their block knocked off. They don't want to get punched. The real winners are stepping in the ring and saying, "fucking *hit* me!" They are trying things all the time. I could tell you I have spent $35,000 or $50,000, or $100,000, and lost it many times. I tested something out and didn't get anything back. No one talks about this because it's not popular. Nobody who is not invested in themselves wants to hear that shit because they are petrified at what happens in that lifestyle, but they also don't want to think about living without millions of dollars. And that is the key that goes back to the decision-making process, the risk-taking process, the mental fortitude that it takes is the dichotomy.

*"This is what it all boils down to on the law of polarity: You can't have the freedoms and the happiness that you want without the discipline that it takes to get there. These are opposites. This is the law of polarity. One doesn't exist without the other."*

This applies to every decision that you make: You have to understand every bad decision that you have made to realize when a good decision is a good decision, or at least have the mental fortitude to make a bad decision and then live with it. If I fucked up, that's okay because I'm going to try again tomorrow. I'm going to fuck up every day of this week because my goal is to find bigger problems to solve. And I know that I can't find them unless I fuck up. I cannot dig those things up unless I make mistakes. If I had led my life without making mistakes, I would have been broke or working at Walmart. How can you live a life without making mistakes? It simply doesn't happen. So you can either live a life of making mistakes broke, or you can live a life of making mistakes and create ample freedom for yourself. Those are your two options.

91

And by the way, it's not about money. You can have financial freedom without being a millionaire. You can have geographical freedom, or freedom of purpose or relationships, or time freedom; you can have all of these things but you still have to be disciplined. We have all heard the story of the mailman who retired after thirty-seven years of service and had $6,000,000 to his name. How do you think that happened? Extreme discipline! That guy created freedoms for himself, and it might not be the roadmap that you want to follow. It's certainly not the roadmap that I want to follow, but you can't disagree that he did it through discipline. Bottom line is that the law of polarity states that if you want the freedoms that you seek, that you desire, that you see all around you, the fast cars, the big house, whatever it is that you want… it's not going to be easy. However, it is possible.

*"When you create the systems and the structure and the support and the team and all those things that go into it, it's freeing."*

It's amazing how you don't even think about the downside and the difficulty because your growth mindset is there, your contribution mindset is there. All I think about all day long is how many seven-figure earners I can make on my team, how many partners I can create that do a million dollars plus each year. How much can I build? How much can I create in my lifetime? I don't have a clue how long I have left, a week, ten days, two days, ten years… no idea! But what can I do while I'm still here? My growth trajectory is how much I can accomplish on Earth. What can I leave behind? What kind of impact can I make?

*"**The Six Human Needs** are very important not just for me and for my style of coaching, but also for people to understand because I don't think they are talked about enough."*

Number one is a **certainty**, which is our need to have foundational roots. It's food, shelter, and water, its safety, its security. It's the understanding that I'm safe and the certainty that everything is around me. It is a basic human need.

Number two is **uncertainty** or **variety**. These are new challenges, playfulness, travel, new experiences, anything that can be different. This could be growth or this could be pushing yourself to another place. Variety, art, hobbies, the works.

Number three is **significance**, which is when we experience rewards. I learned about significance in the military, which is a very interesting place because you go from one pay grade to the next with minuscule increments in pay. But what do they do? They pin you with a new rank, and now all of a sudden, your significance goes up. You're now a petty officer or a second-class petty officer, and your significance goes up in the world. Significance can come from getting a sales reward or being recognized by your peers. We have all experienced that significance somewhere.

Number four is **connection** and **love**. It's kind of self-explanatory as it involves the people around you, your family, your relationships, your spouse or your significant other, the people that make you feel self-love and self-worth, and the things that drive you on a connection level interpersonally.

These top four are the primary needs. These are the basic basics. When we start to go into a depressed state or start to feel like we're sad or we're losing it, or mad or stressed, or that we can't handle it, we have to turn to these top four and ask ourselves what's missing. Where am I falling short? What's wrong? Taking COVID-19 for example, when you're locked into your house for 12 months, I even started to get into a depression state and I realized that it was due to my lack of variety. I like to travel and be outside, to experience things like nature. This lack of variety was hitting me hard, and I consider myself a pretty mentally resilient dude.

Understanding in those top four what's necessary for you to have your basic primary needs met is so important for people. They can either be empowering or disempowering depending on whether or not you're experiencing them. So if you have all four of these met and you're feeling good about them, you have then got that juice. You're confident, your shoulders are back, you feel good about yourself. But if you're missing out on any one of those four, that's when you are having your disempowering days. That's when you feel bad or feel like you're lacking somewhere and can't figure it out. So this is a great checklist to refer back to say that you're feeling kind of funky today and decide to go back to your six human needs to see if there's anything out of place. This is the basics.

Number five is **growth**. And growth for leaders and visionaries – for people who want to play above the line as we call it and become outstanding or extraordinary in their lifetime – can be the pursuit of mastery. That's the learning and teaching and lifelong expanse of your mindset, trying to push to the next level, trying to figure out what is next. Getting feedback from people and learning something new, taking on new experiences and hobbies, and trying to master them. Mastering the Multiplicity Lifestyle and sharing it with your leadership team is a significant part of growth.

Last but not least is **contribution**. Now contribution can take many shapes. It can be as simple as you getting on stage and teaching somebody, volunteering your time, giving back to charity, what you are contributing to society. Growth and contribution are ultimately filling something that we call spiritual needs. These are the things that are going to help elevate you in a self-love, self-worth type of way. They are going to help propel you.

More often than not, if we don't have our primary needs met, we start to rationalize – or tell rational lies – about why it is that we can't fulfill those growth and contribution needs. They'll say they don't have enough time to give back or they can't master anything. They don't listen to podcasts or push themselves to a new level, or they aren't looking for new things to give back to. Why? Because they aren't thinking about others, they're struggling with themselves and their primary needs. It's hard to think about contribution when you don't have self-love. It's hard to think about contribution when you don't have certainty about food, shelter, and water. It's hard to think about a growth mindset when you don't have variety in your life and every day is the same old droll grind. It's hard to think about growth and contribution when you have no significance. Nobody says 'attaboy,' nobody cares, nobody says a good job. Nobody even knows you exist. So why bother pushing to that level, why even go for growth and contribution?

*"It's important to know as a leader and a visionary if you have people on your team who are suffering from this, who are having a hard time giving back or contributing to the team or their community at a high level."*

To take my example as a leader, when we start our meetings on Monday mornings, we start them with what we call "Good News." This is something positive and impactful that's happened to you in the last seven days since we had our last meeting, both personal and business. How did you move the needle in life? When somebody says that nothing happened personally, it can mean two things: One is that they aren't experiencing their primary needs being met because they aren't willing to share or contribute, or two is that they don't trust the group. They don't trust you enough to share.

They might be contributing but they don't trust you and don't want to talk to you about it. It's a very quick temperature check for your team, so whether you have five people on your team or fifty, it only takes two seconds to do a quick "Good News" check-in. Whether it's getting to hang out with your kids down the shore or feeling proud of your team closing great deals last week, that's perfectly good news check-in. And if you can't share that with the team, you have some primary needs issues. It puts you in a good place to start a meeting, setting the tone and the impact that you want to have for this meeting.

This is the positivity that you're going to keep throughout the meeting, not to mention the desired energy level. Excitement creates more excitement, so you're not looking to have someone who brings the rest of them down. If you're bored or depressed, you're going to bring down the temperature of everyone else around you.

Ask yourself this: Why do we walk a little bit taller after a sale? Significance! It's nothing external; it's just that something needs to be fulfilled on the inside. It could be significant because you got rewarded, and it could also be a little bit of variety because money falls into that category, too. Money creates variety. If I give you a big bonus, now you can go do stuff with it. That creates opportunities and not just the same old thing. If you're missing out on all of them or one of them or a couple of them, that is immediately where your depression falls in. It's unfortunate because there are a lot of people who are in some form of depression, and a lot of times it's just this simple.

More often than not, people go into psychological treatment when the answer is right in front of them. All we have to do is run through these six things and see where we fit. Life happens for you, not to you, and this reminder with the six human needs is that everything is happening around you *for* you. It's an impact on you. It's not happening to you, it's not right or wrong, or yes or no, it's all happening for you. So what part are you missing where you can reach out in life and contain that and add it into your six human needs?

*"**Show, share, and grow together** encourages leaders to become more vulnerable with their teams."*

It's all about how we tell stories or how we become vulnerable, and then become teachers and leaders to coach our people. This is one of my favorite things to do: When I'm feeling screwed up or feel like I'm having a bad day because a contract fell apart or someone did me wrong when I'm feeling helpless, I seek ways to be helpful. That's what the law of polarity states. So basically you assist someone else to get your mind off of yourself. Now this can be a lot of different ways like helping an old lady across the street or bringing her groceries in, it could be calling someone up who you know needs a hand, it could be coaching somebody. But this little trick I'm about to tell you takes thirty seconds, and it makes you feel just a little bit uncomfortable but ultimately makes you feel like a million bucks. And that is this: A gratitude video.

I've taught this to thousands of people and I have never once had a single person come back to me to say that it didn't work for them. The only feedback I have ever gotten is how it has changed their lives. The rules are that it must be a video, not a text. Anyone can send a text, but you have to get the emotion behind it. People want to see your face; they want to see how you react, especially post-pandemic where no one has seen anybody for twelve months. They want to see your

99

smiling face. Pick up your smartphone and just make a twenty to thirty-second video, and say why that person is important to you, or what they have done. This can go to your mentors, your team, your salespeople, and people you haven't even met yet. When you send gratitude out there into the ecosystem, whether it gets returned to you in video form or not, it is going to help you. You are going to feel like a rock star. The confidence level that you have is going to go through the roof, and it is going to snap you out of that helpless feeling.

It's giving you a lot of that feeling of those six human needs. It's giving you the certainty that you're safe and you're surrounded by great people that you have in your life. It's a reminder that you have great people, which also relates to connection and love. How many great people do you have in your life who you don't reach out to enough? How many relationships or cousins, aunts, uncles, have truly impacted you, but you haven't even said hi to them in six months? How many people like that are out there? Hundreds! I can think of ten right now off the top of my head while I'm typing this. I don't do this enough even though I do this a lot. So it increases your connection and love, it sure as heck increases your variety and certainty considering that everyone reading this book hasn't done it yet, so it's going to be a new experience for you. And it is going to increase your significance because some of those people are going to be elated and respond to you, telling you how amazing it was and how you've changed their whole day. How you've made their whole week because no one has ever done that for them before. That gives an immediate boost to your significance.

And that's just keeping in mind the four primary needs. Now, you're being taken to the next ecosystem, which is the spiritual needs. Now ask yourself this: Did you get some growth out of that? Is it something that you have never done before? Is it taking you to a new level? Is it something that is pushing you to a new place that you are a little uncomfortable with? I mentioned that earlier that it will feel a little uncomfortable but it is a new thing for you. It's growth. Is it also a contribution? Absolutely. Are you contributing back to other people, is it a societal thing or a tribal thing that you're now saying to them? And if I teach you how to do this, shouldn't you do it for somebody else? That's a contribution. We're touching all six needs in just a thirty-second video.

So when you are feeling helpless, get help. Give back, it will change you. It seems almost impossible considering the first video you do is going to be the hardest. If you're feeling depressed and feel like shit, it's going to be hard to get on video. It's not going to be easy to pick up the phone and tell someone that you appreciate whatever it is they have done for you. But you start with one and it turns into two, then three. I generally do twenty videos and I'll do it till I feel better. Don't expect a return out of it or expect them to get back to you with another video. They'll just text you back because they're shocked wondering what they did. Maybe they'll call you asking why you sent them that video. Try it, it works; that's my response.

And don't even think about keeping score. The great people who are doing great things don't keep score. They just keep doing and doing what serves them and others. The only score you are keeping is what you are giving out and the value that you are creating.

"The more you care, the stronger you can be."

**Jim Rohn**

That's the amount of income that you will make: How much value you create for others. It's not a one-for-one thing. I don't create value for you today and you immediately write me a check. Sometimes I add and I add and I add value to you for years and maybe you'll hire me as a coach in six months or five years. Maybe one day they'll understand how much you've been impacting them that they decide they will hire you. I don't expect that to happen the first time we meet, and it's the same thing with this gratitude video. You can't expect to send someone a thirty-second video and suddenly wake up to your importance in their life that way. But ultimately, you will open doors with this thing.

# Chapter 8

# Great Leaders Create Great Leaders

**Multiplicity is ABUNDANT; what's learned is shared, passed on in your words, with your stories.**

*"It all starts with you."*

This is after years of masterminding and group coaching and everybody wanting to buy in or grow or start a team that they can delegate all their shit to. I think it is one of the biggest, cancerous things in a society where people think they can start a company and get a bunch of people to come work for them and they can then hand it off to them. I was that guy. That was me six years ago. That was the first team that I started. So when I was in the Superman story phase of my life, the transition from that was that I had to let go of the vine and trust people to do stuff which in itself is difficult to do. The transition begins generally from being everything to everyone and not ready to delegate things to anyone because nobody can do it better, to giving something to someone to do and they did it and they didn't blow it up, even did it better. So why not give them some more stuff to do. Then it becomes almost like a drug that you can do that, give others things to do and you start to grow. And what happens with that drug is that it becomes addictive, especially in the real-estate game.

When you have a business that you can print money, and you can scale it quickly, and make a lot of cash, you start to become a product of your problems. You start to make enough cash for hiring more people to solve the problems. If I had that couldn't be processed, I hired processors. I woke up one morning and I had processors processing for processors. I asked one what they were processing and their answer was filed. Okay, so how many deals did we close this month? Two. Two? Did you work for a team that closed just two deals this month? Stop the madness! And I realized that we were just throwing bodies at problems instead of being good leaders. And that is part of what made me reset the clock. And when I say part of it, the real reason was the culture. Of course, I didn't like the culture and I didn't like being the leader of a piss-poor culture. I didn't like being surrounded by people that I didn't love, and of course, I didn't like the inefficiencies around me. But it got back to me realizing that I had to own my shit. I had to be a good leader. I couldn't be that asshole who would walk around talking about firing people, or walking around like I didn't have to be there, or like my shit didn't stink and I didn't have to do any work because I was the CEO. Probably the worst title in the world, even though I carry it in some of my companies.

You can be a CEO and still lead from the front. Leading from the back is the worst place to lead. Nobody who leads from the back is a good leader. It's impossible. You can't point at people and tell them what to do unless you're willing to do it. Or better yet, show them how it's done and carry yourself at a level that you want them to carry themselves at. You can't tell people to read books and listen to podcasts if you are not doing it yourself. You can't tell people to educate themselves and listen to podcasts instead of spending time on Netflix if *your* ass is on Netflix forty hours a week. You can't tell people to get up at 5 am and go to the gym if you haven't been in the gym in five years. You can't do these things if you are not doing them.

So the first thing is that it starts with you. And that is what I call visionary shit for a reason. If you are not being a visionary, and you are not learning it from the top, and you are not growing it from the top, and you are not being it from the top, then you cannot expect them to be it. You cannot expect them to be leaders because you are not showing them how to be leaders. I use this analogy with my daughters all the time as for a long time; all parents experience this on some level. People think that if they tell their kids enough times, they might get it. They don't! They don't get it unless they experience you doing it and that they see you enough times.

You can yell at your kids all you want, but it isn't going to change anything. But when you show them what it is like to be a good person, when you show them what it is like to eat well, when you show them what it is like to stay hydrated and drink water all the time. My kids used to joke about it but I listen to podcasts at 2X speed because it is a life hack: You consume knowledge twice as fast. They think it is a joke but they *do* it. They will come in the bathroom when I am playing podcasts at 2X speed and they will listen to them. Now that I have done it so many times, they are dialed in. Even while they are 8 and 11, I am positive that when they start listening to educational podcasts ten years from now, this is how they are going to do it. I don't have to get up early on a Sunday morning, but sometimes I will get up at 4 a.m. on a Sunday and go watch the sunrise at the beach. Our house is near the bay and I have to walk a half-mile to the beach or ride my bike there, and I will just go there to watch the sunrise. Well, last year, my daughter surprised me at 3:45 am, and she came into my room and wanted to go with me. She was all dressed up and ready to go with me to watch the sunrise. I was blown away! I didn't ask her to do it, but because she saw me doing it enough times, it triggered her and she woke herself up. She just got out of bed and came to get me, so we walked down to the beach to watch the sunrise together. All because she saw it enough times, and that just proves that you can be a good leader if they see it enough times, and they will believe. That is how you become a visionary: You show people the way, with a clear Vision and big Story.

The second piece of it is so impactful and empowering, because if you don't have a big story and a belief in your big story and you don't share it, then nobody knows your big story. You have to be passionate about your big story.

When I talk about storage, I'm scared to death half the time. But you will never know it. Our vision now is that I am doing twenty deals this year whether it freaking kills us, and I'm surrounded by the best team of professionals in the country to do it with. We have the best JV partners, we have the best sites, we are underwriting fifty deals to buy two, we are doing all the work and spending tens of thousands of dollars to do the underwriting on each deal, we are cherry-picking off-market deals. We have gone out of our way to make sure that we are buying in the fastest-growing markets so that we can have the leverage and the ability to beat our competition to the best spots in America. When I tell you that, do you want to be on that ride with me or not? You're damn right you do because I have that passion behind me.

Do you know how many self-storage deals I own right now? Four. But I have the passion and the vision to own twenty this year. I sound like a guy who owned twenty, five years ago. The truth is that I am three years into being the storage guy at this level because it has taken that long of due diligence and learning and growth and push and investors. The first deal took eighteen months to buy and get approvals for and whatnot. That is all bullshit and drama, but the reality of it is that it took us two deals in. It took us three years to buy two deals. But now is the rocket fuel. Now we have amazing partners. We have the best partners in the country, the best engineers, the best designers, the best material suppliers.

And when I say the best, I'm not just blowing smoke up your ass. I mean the best! We source the best people. My chief development officer has built over three hundred self-storage facilities and this guy knows everybody in the industry. Our third-party management teams are the best. It's three of the top five operators in the country; we know the directors of all those companies and we are talking with them directly. We have built relationships with the best of the best of the best, and we have done it in three years. Now, I have the confidence level to say that we are going to kill it and we are just on the ground floor. That is being a visionary. People want to follow you when you have that confidence behind you,

And that confidence comes from clarity, which goes back to COIs and RPMs. If I don't know my purpose, and if I don't know the outcome that I am looking to achieve, and if I don't know why I am doing it, then I cannot be that confident when I talk about it. My purpose is to build a team of people that I love, that I can create real wealth and a real legacy with because twenty-five years from now those people will still be in my life and they will be wealthy as a result. My purpose is that my joint-venture partners all retire younger and have better lives and better families because they do business with us. My purpose is that my investors that come along for the ride get to make money four different ways, and they get to get equity in these deals, and they get to get paid big-time on the backside. And that they get to be involved and they love it because they are a part of the deal with us. It is part of my impact and part of our purpose. That is what juices me up, and you can feel the passion when I talk about it. Again, that is all part of being a visionary. You have to package that up and you have to own it.

So, it all starts with you. If you don't have *that* dialed in, you cannot expect people to follow you. And I don't care what it is that you do, by the way. You could be the best cake baker and you need to be that passionate about cakes. We've all seen Carlo's Bake Shop on TV, and that man is that passionate about cakes in the shapes of cars. I could never do that! Every one of us is a genius. That is the whole point of what we are trying to say here: You can multiply no matter what you do. And every single person reading this book is perfect the way they are. What I mean by that is that you have greatness in you already. You are already a genius at something. Forget about your negative past. Forget about what you have been telling yourself. Forget about the limiting beliefs that have been holding you back. Forget about what people think about you. Forget about the inner voice and the rational lies that you are telling yourself. If I asked you right now what you are truly fucking amazing at, just pretend that you are in a quiet room by yourself and nobody is listening and you are only answering that question to yourself.

Just admit to yourself what you are truly amazing at, and something is going to come out. Go with the first thing that you can think of because remember, if you were to flip a quarter, you already know what you are wishing for before it even hits your hand. You know what you are great at. So what are you already a genius at? Because everyone reading this book already has that in them. You may be an amazing gymnast, an amazing cake baker, great at repairing cars, great at welding, great at real estate, or maybe you are a great orator. Les Brown has made millions and millions of dollars just by talking.

So many people get paid to do what they love, and I think that is what is missed in life. Sure, this is a great debate that goes back decades and decades where people argue that you cannot get paid to do what you love. I think that is bullshit. I think you have to find your passion and figure out how you get paid doing that, and I think that you also get concentrated on doing it. Whether you do it nights and weekends, part-time, or just do it for fun, in front of people, or you teach people how to do it. Here's the thing about the knowledge business right now: People are getting paid to do the dumbest shit. Last night, I was in bed thinking what the number one thing that is holding me back from my fitness right now: Stretching. I'm not flexible. I'm lifting more weight than I ever have in my entire life but I'm limited by my range of motion.

I'm putting weight over my head that I couldn't bench press when I was twenty-five. But I am not flexible. So ironically, I was flipping through Facebook last night, and what do I find? Some dude who put together a course on stretching. Fucking stretching! This guy's genius is stretching; he is a genius at stretching. Think about that. I open the Video Sales Letter (VSL) but I don't want to watch it, I go right to the order button. There is a seventeen-page long copy on testimonials and comments, out of which I look at the first five comments that say stuff like it is the best thing in stretching that has ever happened, or this thing is a life-changer... great! Buy now! $37, it's in my cart, it's on my card, done! Bought the stretching video. This dude is selling videos on stretching. Think about that. If he is not making well over six figures a year, I will be highly surprised. I didn't even Google stretching, the Facebook ad was right there.

If you cannot find your genius, spend time thinking on that, journaling on that, paying attention to that, because every one of us has genius inside of us.

To come up with the solution, you must understand the problem. The next step to being a great leader is good feedback. Most leaders start, especially at the very beginning, with do, do, do. Here's the SOP, here's how it should be done, go out there and do it, let me know when it is done, get back to me when it is done. If you want to accelerate the learning curve or take a quantum leap as a leader, do the opposite. Seek good feedback or ask better questions. Instead of telling, ask for feedback. Not a day goes by that I am not on the phone with someone from my team asking them what is working for them right now, what is not working, and what they think we should be doing. A couple of different things happen psychologically there. Number one is your team is begging for your attention, and that is all positive attention. When you ask somebody questions, what happens?

It gets them deep into their psyche, but it also gets them heard. People want to speak and be heard and know that you are interested in them. If I am just telling you something, I am giving you attention for sure but I am just dumping on you. But if I am asking you, all of a sudden I care. By the way, I cannot ask you questions without caring unless

I'm just not paying attention to what you are saying. If you give me feedback and I am not writing it down or paying attention to you, then I am an asshole. There is a fine balance here: You have to ask these questions with intention and pay attention. So when you ask the questions, ask them with sincerity. What is going on today, what is working for you, what is not working for you, what do you think we should change, what do you think we should do differently, what are we not doing that we should be doing? Get that feedback from them.

So I am constantly seeking feedback from all members of my team, not giving feedback. If I give feedback, which is super rare, I'm always giving negative and leaving with a positive. If I have to give them negative feedback, I'm going to leave them with an uplift. I might say that I noticed how they handled something and would like to give some feedback. If it is related to a call, I might point out that they missed out on some questions inside the script, and I will point out why they are super important and how they will improve the close ratio. I know that sometimes when I made these calls, I missed that question right there. For example, we ask the seller how they rate the house on a scale of one to ten. I know it sounds like a super silly question, but let me explain to you why that question is so important and impactful. If a seller comes back to you and says their house is a ten, I love to get back to them and point out how it's a ten after they mentioned that it needs a new kitchen and the roof is shot. What would you give if they were new? If I asked on a scale of one to ten, would you give it a fifteen if they were new? Because I want to build rapport and make them laugh. That gives you an *in* to get them to laugh or to get them to engage with you. I might also mention to the person who I am giving feedback that they mentioned how they were having trouble building rapport, so if they miss some of these little questions which sound silly, that might be there to build rapport. So if they are missing the rapport piece, that might be the reason why. I also highlight how they are kicking ass and I love what they are doing, I just wanted to give them that feedback because I noticed it. Always leave them on a positive note, which again was not me about five to seven years ago.

*"Back then, I would just yell, yell, yell, eat em up, beat em up, push em down; that was the old me. The new me is more, 'Hey, look. Here's the deal. Here's what we need to get done, and I trust that you own your seat and your role. So let me know if I can be of any assistance, and I appreciate you doing what you are doing.'"*

Trust and respect, which ultimately leads to delegation. Or more importantly, delegate to elevate. When I delegate things, a lot of people look at delegation as condescension. They believe that if I delegate something to you, it's as if I am throwing my crap at you. But it is the opposite. A lot of people will delegate to micromanage, for instance delegating something to someone and then telling them to check back every fifteen minutes till it is done, or they will stand over you till it is done. That is the opposite of good leadership. Here is what a good delegation looks like. It is telling them that you want them to do something and then asking them honestly if they are capable of doing it. If they aren't, they should be upfront about it because you want to set good expectations so that you are both on the same page. You can also offer them any points where they need help. Because you trust them and know that they are going to own their role, so you can also ask for an approximate time that it will take to finish.

You have to trust the people you delegate to. I would not even check in with that person, or if I did, I might just ask if they needed anything. That's it: Support. Not hassling the person hours before the end of the day and trying to get an update if it is 80% done yet. That just destroys people because they want to be in an environment where they are being supported. Think about this like you are on a Super Bowl team. If you had Super Bowl A-level players in there who were rock stars, and their job was to go out there to catch every ball and bring it down. Their team was 100% behind them because they knew their talents were top-notch. These were the best of the best. Every time that dude went to practice and missed a catch for whatever reason, the team

wouldn't go about telling him things like, "You asshole! I can't believe you didn't catch that ball. What the hell are you going to do in the game on Sunday? Holy shit, butterfingers, I hope you bring the heat on Sunday. If you play as you did in practice, we're screwed." Do you think that a Superbowl team does that shit? Not! What does a Superbowl team do? They support every single player no matter what. It could be the third quarter down by 30 and somebody screws up. They do everything in their power to be like, "It doesn't matter, we still got you. Let's go. You'll get it next time. Shake it off."

*"It's support, support, support, and that is your job as a visionary: To make them feel like you tell your story. Make them feel like your passion. We have to transfer our outcome and our results, and they have to have the same thing. So when I say 'Show, Share and Grow,' that is what I am talking about."*

If you have a result and outcome, and you have a COI and RPM, guess what? Everyone on your team has to have the same thing. They need to grow and learn. They need to understand it, need to have it explained to them, the same way that I just explained it to you. And they need to buy into it as if it is part of their culture. For example, every Thursday morning at 9:45, I have what I call the Mastermind call for my team. Right now, I have three companies. It is all executive-level or management-level people, or even my partners, from those three teams on that call. If you hit a certain level in my company, you are invited to be on that call, and we talk about mindset stuff, about COIs, about growth, about things that rob your energy, about the things that keep your mindset straight, about your passion, about your results. We talk about your family, about keeping everything in alignment, about gratitude, about wealth creation, about the saboteurs, about the Five Freedoms, about everything. I give it all away and we eliminate the scarcity mindset so that I can breathe into them the abundance that I want to have in my life, and therefore they can do the same to their people, to their tribes, to their families, and everyone that they come in contact with. I want them on the phone talking to my JV partners the way I am talking to them. I want them on the phone talking to brokers and our engineers, our third-party teams, our clients, and our customers. I want them to talk to their sales teams and everyone that they come into contact with at the same level that I am talking to them.

That is a Tribe of Leaders. Just think about this for a second. A tribe, or a common group of people after a common mission, doing certain things together. They think they believe, they feel the same way, so doing this Mastermind call every Thursday gets people to think not just about business, but about themselves, their health, how they are going to solve problems or handle problems, or how they are going to handle their teams when problems happen. All of a sudden, it's not just about business, but rather about the overall complete package of the human being which is, guess what, going to elevate those people around them. Therefore, everyone has a common mission and they are all going up at the same time. Because I do not want people on that call who aren't doing that shit. That is not my tribe then.

One of my guys recently brought to the table his personal best and his business best. This is a guy who came from the auto industry, would work nights, weekends, every holiday of the year, and also has two young kids. After he came to work for me, he has made more money than he has ever made in his entire life, has more freedom than he has ever had in his entire life, and is now the leader of one of my companies. His personal best was carving out two hours in the middle of the workday to take his kids sledding. That was what he said in front of the whole company and everyone was like "He did what? How the hell are you going to let that happen?" Let it happen? I told him to do it! That is called time freedom. When you can get done with what you are supposed to get done and go sledding with your kids, that's a win-win. That is the creation of time freedom. For anybody that knows, it's freaking dark at 4 o'clock. When is he supposed to take his kids' sledding? Go do it at noon! The kids are homeschooled, they get done at noon, and that is when you go sledding.

*"This is not weird shit, this is leadership. This is visionary shit. This is creating great leaders. I want leaders that are not afraid to go take their kids sledding at 2 pm."*

Leaders that are not afraid to create an environment where getting your COIs done in the middle of the day is not going to interrupt getting your business COIs done whenever the hell they fit in your calendar. That's the difference. I will yell at somebody on my team for not going home for family dinner. I will yell at someone on my team if they are in the office at 9 p.m. for more than two nights in a row because I know at that point that they are not being productive for themselves and they are not being productive for their families. They are not helping us as a team. They are not being good for their team members or their tribe around them if they are burning themselves out trying to get a business goal done. I can immediately tell you when one of my guys is in the office late multiple nights in a row that they are fucking slipping up on their stuff. So I have to step in as a leader and remind them to get a grip and tell them to go spend time at home with their wife. I know they are missing that piece and it is not creating a good balance. It is a different type of leadership and a different type of culture.

I hear these people talking about golden handcuffs and having a crazy 401K that they cannot leave their job for. The

119

truth of the matter is one of the things I have learned during the transition of COVID-19, that all of that stuff is complete BS. People will leave a job like that and take a pay cut to come and work at a place with a better culture. Not that we pay less, but I have had people coming and saying they will work with a better culture no matter what I'm paying because they do not want the environment that they are in. No one has ever called them a leader before. No one has ever helped them grow before. No one has ever given a shit about their kids before. No one has ever told them that there were Five Freedoms, let alone how to create them. No one has ever helped them grow as a person before.

They were treated like a number. Humans are not resources or fuel that you just burn them up and spit them out. These people are your team. We have to continue to renew them and keep them energized, and keep their part of the team, and grow with them. They are not renewable energy. So we have to stop treating people as racehorses and start treating them like part of the family.

One of the core values of our business is what I call **70% is a Go**. This is part of the delegation, of accountability, of responsibility, part of training people to make mistakes. This is probably one of the biggest things that helps people become leaders that I see people mistakes about all the time and it gets back to problem-solving. It solves so many issues in one core value. I hear people say that you can't train accountability, or that people have to be accountable for themselves before they come to work for you. It's all horseshit. I don't know who came up with that theory but it drives me fucking nuts when I hear it. The problem is that people have never been given responsibility before, and then held accountable. When they are not held accountable or given responsibility, they become spoiled kids. Imagine if you have a super spoiled child that you just gave everything to all the time, and then they grew up as a brat. Guess what? Of course, they are not going to be responsible or accountable for anything because you have been spoiling them their whole life without holding them accountable for anything. You've been babying them and giving them candy, bought them their first car, and whatnot.

The best people that I have found in life were the ones who had discipline growing up, or the ones who were forced to make decisions, or the ones who were forced to solve problems. They were the kids who got dirty, got into fistfights, who didn't get participation trophies for showing up. I wrestled in 142 weight class and there were seven of us in the goddamn weight class. I sucked at wrestling because I could never compete in a seven-division weight class. But I took my lumps and I got through life because I fought the whole time. I look back on that and it is part of what gave me the integrity and the energy, and defined who I am. It built character. The problem is that when you treat your people like spoiled brats and you don't give them responsibility, then they don't become accountable.

I say all that to say this: 70% is a Go. In our team, if you are 70% sure, you take action. If you are 70% sure of something and you have to ask what you should do, I'm not going to answer your question because I'm going to ask you what we should do. Are you 70% sure? Then what the fuck are you bringing it to me for? Go! Do it! And here is the catch-22 as a leader: You cannot have this rule in place, and then yell at your people when they screw up. Because people are going to make mistakes when you have this rule in place. They are going to go out, make a decision because they are 70% sure, and they are going to fall on their face. Your job as a great visionary at this point is to pick them up, dust them off, say "good job for making a decision, now go out there and do it again."

*"You are an entrepreneur at some point in time, you still are. Every day, you decide because there is no one else to make these decisions. It could be a $10,000 decision or a $100,000 decision, or even a $1,000,000 decision. You fucked up, you had no one else to blame because this is your vision, and you got better and you made a better decision tomorrow because of it."*

If you want leaders on your team, you have to train them to do the same thing. If you screwed up and there was no one to yell at you, then you are not allowed to yell at them. If they screw up and you yell at them, what are they going to do next time? They are not going to make a decision anymore. They are going to be paralyzed with fear. You are going to teach them that solving problems is not something that you tolerate anymore. You are going to teach them that if they screw up and you yell at them, what are they going to do the next time? Come to you for the answers. You are going to train people that they cannot solve problems without coming to you first for the answers. It is the antithesis of what you want. You can't have all these employees coming to you for all the answers. That's not who you are training. You're training leaders, not betas! You want people who know how to go out there and solve problems. You might think you are fixing the problem but you are creating another problem because now they are not going to make a decision, and they are going to lean on you to only decide after you give them approval, which is going to slow up your momentum personally.

We already saw in Controlling the Clock that if someone comes to me with a problem, they need to come to me with three solutions. As a leader, you have to make a practice, make a promise, and set a standard within yourself right here and now that you will not correct issues without asking them how they would solve them. If you, at that level, are 70% sure that the resolution is even remotely doable, let them do it. And when I say remotely, I mean if it can even scratch the surface of being possibly doable. Here's the biggest problem: People come back and say they have a solution, and you say it's okay but you would do it another way, you give them a micro-managed solution to an issue which will make them doubt themselves and their problems solving skills more, resulting in them coming back to you for a solution every time. So if they start to come back to you with a solution, let them go for it!

*"Unless they are giving you a solution that is going to implode the company, let them go for it. Let's say it baubles or bumbles or implodes a little bit and they fail, they are going to come back to you to tell you their solution failed. Well, you learned a lesson. Try again next time."*

Now they know that it is on their shoulders, and they can either be the victor or the victim. You do not ever want to be their savior. You want to be their support structure and you want to be the guy who is holding them up, dusting them off, and making them feel good about themselves and about making decisions. Not the one giving them the answer, not being their solution-ist, not being their victor, but allowing them to be the victor. They need to be the hero.

124

When you teach people that they can be stopped when you teach people that their solutions are wrong, or you teach people that their ideas are bad, what happens? I meditate with my daughter and I tell her she is strong, she is powerful, she is amazing, she is beautiful, and she is going to rule the world. Just whisper these things in their ear constantly and what do they do? They start to think that. It's no different than your people and your team. They need to believe this stuff, so why not repeat that? Why not help them believe that? If you become their chief problem solver, you're training betas. You don't want followers, you want leaders. We talk about A, B, and C players, and I want all A-players. When you are surrounded by A-players, A-players want to be surrounded by A-players. If you go on a Mastermind yacht, everyone on that yacht is an A-player. They are getting on that yacht to be surrounded by A-players. And when somebody hates on that experience, those are C-players. These people are allergic to A-players. They talk shit, they are negative, they hate on it, they don't understand it, they don't want to be a part of it, why would they even spend the money to do that, that's silly, that's bullshit. They are selling themselves on their story about why doing that is crazy because of all kinds of excuses.

*"The people who think that money is the root of all evil have never given away enough money."*

**Mark Evans DM**

When you are on that yacht, you're thinking about how you can create such an impact with the money you have made that you can feed a thousand people, or create opportunities for homeless veterans, or take guide dogs and give them to blind people. You are creating an impact on that yacht. C-players don't even think about that because they are so stuck in their mind and so focused on the four primary needs that Contribution and Growth haven't even entered their mind. They are worried about not worrying about their paycheck every Friday or about paying their student loans or the mail coming in that says, "Past Due."

They are more concerned with not worrying about their health and safety, or their landlord kicking them out. They are only worried about one through four of the Six Human Needs. So C-players are allergic to A-players, while A-players are attracted to A-players. As for B-players, they have one of two options available to them. The first thing that can happen to them is that they get inspired and start to grow towards the A-players and take on their habits, their story, their state, their standard, and want to push themselves to that level to

126

become an A-player. And then they start to hang out with the A-players and the next thing you know, they become more A than they were B. Or the second option where they listen to all the negative bullshit and they become like crabs in a bucket. They listen to all the negativity of a C-player and bring the B-players down to their level. I don't want to hang out with C-players, don't even want to be near them. So my team will be all As because that's who I want to hang out with. Those are the people who I love. When I am on the phone with them, they inspire me, they push me.

That's the dichotomy: When you create a tribe of leaders, they are all As. They are all fucking As, every single one of them. The truth is that I believe C-players are cancer in your company, but I also believe that A-players are pretty much immune to it. When you get to the point where you are at an outstanding or extraordinary level, where you play above the line all day and every day, you block C-players out. You don't even hear them anymore. It is kind of like with social media, if I see the negativity, I block. There is no feeling about it whatsoever because they don't even exist to A-players anymore. So I believe the C-player has a major effect on a B-player because they don't know right or wrong, or which direction to go. But to an A-player, it's irrelevant.

That's a bulletproof mindset that allows you to not care. And you know what happens then? The people who do belong and want to belong, and they do feel about what you are putting out there are attracted to you like magnets.

# Conclusion (with one rule)

This is a big shift for me that I have experienced in the last two years. I realized that I spent seven years creating masterminds and 'coaching' and events and stuff around real-estate investors, and what I realized after doing that for all of these years was that we didn't teach real estate. Not saying we didn't teach real estate, of course, we did. But 85% of what we taught was about mindset, keeping your shit together, hiring great people, and so on. We talked about being a good leader and a good coach, creating opportunities for others.

*"Ultimately what multiplicity is, is putting all those things together and creating multiple effects. Because now we're creating a tribe of great leaders, or what I would like to call **'great leaders creating great leaders.'"***

I'm talking about spawning off these great leaders within my organization which ultimately start to multiply themselves and they create more great leaders because that is the culture that we foundationally create from day one.

And so these things that we've talked about for about five to seven years now in real-estate masterminds have now created this opportunity where I've eliminated all of them. I have gotten rid of the group coaching space mostly because people hide in groups. And I found out that when I have a bunch of people in a room, I can speak and put my energy into them and go all in, and ultimately, they can *still* fail. Because when you ask a group of ten people to talk about their problems, maybe one person will raise their hand for a surface-level issue like "I had a hard time closing a sale this week." Sure, let's talk about that. Meanwhile, one of those people is falling apart internally and will never say what's going on inside them. They will never raise their hand out of a deathly fear that the group is going to judge them while thinking "what a loser, did you spend the last week curled up in a ball on your couch crying, while I'm over here kicking ass and taking names…"

So what happens is that in a group, we hide. This is why I have completely transitioned over to one-on-one coaching; it is all I do now. Of course, I do events and other gatherings but they will be invite-only or super-private, completely unadvertised. You might see me going to Vale in two weeks, but no one is ever going to be told about it. It will mostly be my partners and executives and my team, which is where my group coaching lies now: With my partners. I don't even charge for that. But with one-on-one coaching, I can get deep into it. We laugh, we cry, we freaking shout at each other like it's about creating a real impact and doing, what I like to call, collapsing time. It's a six-month program, a thirty-six in six, which means that I am doing three years' worth of time collapsing in six months. But it's all of these things that I've learned that aren't real-estate-based. These are all growth and trajectory and legacy oriented, what is it that I am trying to create and why.

*"In fifteen years of real estate, I've made every sort of mistake there can be under the sun. Now it's like I'm on the warpath for the next ten years, and I want to share that with people."*

**Multiplicity** is not going to be a course or a speech that I'm going to be putting out, it is going to be dealing with one-on-one coaching. And this is completely no-holds-barred: I'm giving it all away here. I want people to read this and go "dude, this was incredible! I want more of this!" It's going to have all of the things I would talk about one-on-one. It is geared towards business owners and entrepreneurs not just limited to those in real estate.

Naturally, we can help those people get on a trajectory to get to where they're trying to go a lot quicker, but ultimately this can be doctors, attorneys, chiropractors, etc. No specific industry, it could be anyone willing to make six figures or more in their life and they have some sort of established base that they can use as a launchpad. It's not your typical 9-to-5 grind though it could be as I've coached people in that space as well. But it is for people who want to create teams and growth and create a contribution out of their life.

131

A lot of the stuff that I have implemented myself in the last couple of years has made such a massive impact in my life that I believe that I have a moral obligation to share this stuff because it works. I don't teach theory, I'll never teach something that I just read and didn't do. I have done everything that I'm saying to you today, and I believe that once people understand this and implement it in practice, they are going to have an obligation to share it with their team. It's a part of being a great leader who is going to create great leaders: You have to share this stuff, you can't keep it in. And that is the multiplicity factor. It's going to multiply only if you use it. You're only going to create a tribe of leaders if you become a leader, and the only way that you are going to become a leader is if you implement the process.

## One rule

Remember how I told you there is only one rule by reading this book? **The only way the process works is if you share it.** That's it. That is the rule. It can be anyone that you come in contact with not just limited to your team. You can share this with your kids, I do coaching sessions with my kids and I teach them this. My eleven-year-old daughter has a whiteboard that she fills out every Sunday morning and I teach her these lessons. This stuff works with everyone if you share it, and it makes you a better person and a better leader every time you share it.  The key to unlocking freedom is to multiply what works for you in those around you.

Once free, stay free.

-   Joe

Made in the USA
Middletown, DE
14 August 2021